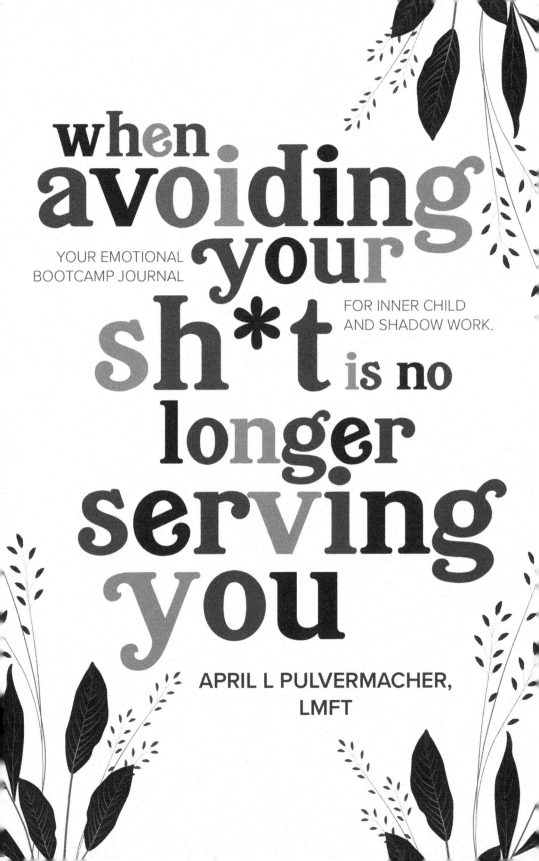

when
avoiding
your

YOUR EMOTIONAL
BOOTCAMP JOURNAL

FOR INNER CHILD
AND SHADOW WORK.

sh*t is no
longer
serving
you

APRIL L PULVERMACHER, LMFT

When Avoiding Your Sh*t Is No Longer Serving You
©April Pulvermacher

Print ISBN 979-8-35092-460-2
eBook ISBN 979-8-35092-461-9

preface

This book is for all the people out there that knew they needed something more, but didn't know what. Knew they needed to start somewhere, but didn't know where. Knew they needed to change something, but didn't know how. Knew something wasn't quite right, but didn't know why.

I created this book because I knew there was a need for it when some of my clients didn't know how to start journaling, or what to write, or they finally picked out the perfect notebook and pen, but then they didn't want to write in the book because, "What if I ruin it or do it wrong?". *Face palm*

So here, now both the questions and the paper are all in one spot. No need to search for the perfect notebook or to stare at blank pieces of paper anymore. Just start. It might take a bit to find the best pen for the job, though, because we all know writing with that favorite pen makes all the difference. However, once that's done, hop to it and chop chop.

acknowledgments

Thank you for everyone who has given me the strength to keep getting up each day. Thank you to my friends and family that have supported me through all the bullshit that life has thrown my way. A special shout out to my dad for helping sponsor this writing endeavor and for my mom who is watching my back from above. I will always be grateful for everything ya'll have taught and done for me. Thank you to my fur babies and your unconditional love, cuddles, kisses, and laughs while writing this thing. Finally, a BIG thank you to all of my beautiful clients that have helped me grow into a better therapist and person each and every day. You are the real MVP's and I love watching ya'll succeed and heal in life.

You are my people, the misfits and the underdogs. We were put on this Earth to support one another while experiencing life for all that is has to give, so keep kicking ass and taking names!

contents

chapter 1

W E L C O M E

Hello friends! I can only imagine what adventures you've been through to get yourself here, reading this lovely book. I do hope there's been nothing too traumatic, however I have a feeling it's bad enough since it's come to this point. This journal is a tool to use for your healing journey and help you answer some questions you may have had floating around in that beautiful little skull of yours. You can use it however you'd like. You can either pick it up, answer a couple questions, put it down, and pick it up months later, or you can create a routine and fill out a page each day for the year. Granted, the later could help you gain momentum and some semblance of enlightenment as to why you are the way you are because the effort you put into this journey is what you'll be getting out of it. Kind of like going to the gym. You can go there once a month just to say you went, but if you're expecting those 6 pack abs directly afterwards, you'll be highly disappointed. However, if you go regularly and apply better eating habits throughout the week, you might just start seeing results sooner, rather than later. So this process is totally up to you. Just know it only works if you actually do it.

I will be the first to admit that I am awful at being consistent with day to day tasks and the goals I've set in my life. "I will start working out tonight while I'm watching my show," my overly ambitious morning self tells me. Then later that night, I'm staring at the resistance bands laying in a basket in the corner while I'm sitting my happy ass on the couch with my cat on my lap, my dog laying next to me, and binge watching whatever show I'm into at the moment.

It's a process! Progress is not linear, your best looks different every day, and it may contain some pauses, backwards steps, and huge gains... and that's OK! There are no "should's" or "have to's" here, only "could's" and "when you're ready's". Trust yourself, trust this adventure is yours and yours alone, and finally, trust the process.

The work starts with you. No one else. At some point, blaming other people will no longer be working and you'll be fed up with the shit you have been avoiding enough to decide to do something differently. Luckily for you, I'm not even asking you to change your life, or to pick up those judgey resistance bands collecting dust in the corner, I'm really not even asking you to do anything if I'm being honest. You're the one that picked this book. You're the one that has been experiencing some kind of stress or emotional block that has had you googling, "How do I make this shit go away?" and Tada! Your wish is my command, or Google's, I suppose. For others, this book might have fallen into your lap by either a gift or some other serendipitous occurrence and now you're reading it and thinking something along the lines of, "What did I get myself into now?".

You're Welcome!!! (Sang in Maui's voice) I invite you to your emotional bootcamp journey. This is where you will be asked questions that may or may not bring some uncomfortable emotions up to the surface. One of the things I've learned while working with these questions is that, usually, your first initial answer to the question is your ego talking. It's the safe answer; the one with fluff, sounds good, and feels comfortable. (Keep Going!) The next few sentences you write will have you reluctantly getting a little deeper into the meat and potatoes of your soul. Finally, once you get into sentence 6 to whichever, you finally start diving into the philosophical aspects and connecting some dots. This is where you want to be. This is where the healing is. This is where you can really lean into some uncomfortable truths, thoughts, and feelings and then work through them. When you can get comfortable sitting in the uncomfortable, you will be able to find patterns from your past to your present. That's where you can learn to forgive the people who raised you and yourself so you'll finally be able to release, let go, and evolve into a more healthy version of yourself. You'll find some examples of this in chapter 4. Also, some questions might resonate with you more than others, which just makes sense. Everyone has a different story and I wouldn't expect someone to have the same draw or reservations to each question. Go where your intuition takes you. On the flip side, if you read a question and notice an instant, "Whoa, this has nothing to do with my X, Y, Z." or "That's a dumb question, I don't know what that has anything to do with blah blah blah..." then those are the questions that need the most attention. You feeling defensive to the question is telling you where there is resistance in your body, and that's where the healing is critical.

For the record, I'm not going to throw you head first into the shallow end of the community pool without at least providing you with some floaties and a helmet, I'm not THAT mean. Plus, how else am I going to get word of mouth referrals for this book if you get head trauma? The goal for this journey is to be healing and enlightening, not retraumatizing. With that being said, if, for any reason during this adventure, you find yourself in a come to Jesus moment and are feeling too overwhelmed, please reach out to a local therapist or counselor. That way you can pause and really dive into some of the traumas that are coming up while in a more supportive and con-trolled environment. You are not alone in your mess and you should never have to feel like you need to deal with it by yourself. (Because that's called hyper-independence and is also a trauma response. So, yea, there's that sprinkle of information for ya.)

In the meantime, there is a chapter with a few helpful coping skills that you may want to utilize if anything becomes a little too intense. You can even practice said coping skills instead of punch-ing that annoying coworker that can't keep their nose out of every one's business in the face, or if the car in front of you is going the EXACT speed limit and you're cursing them out with all types of names that would have your grandma blushing, or even if your child has screamed "Look at me! Look at me!" for the 100th time and you want to yell back, "I don't fucking care!". These skills are here to help keep you sane, safe, and silent so you don't cuss out the boss and quit in the middle of a Tuesday afternoon meeting that could have very easily been an email.

So, buckle up, go at your own pace, enjoy the ride, and may the odds be ever in your favor.

chapter 2

BRAIN INFO

Why use coping skills? What do they even do? Are they just a bunch of "woo woo" activities people talk about in theory or do they actually work in reality? Well, here's what science has taught us and here's what I've learned that has been successful for me and for the other people I've worked with. Coping skills are activities you can do to help regulate your brain and circulatory system when you're stressed out, or "triggered". When you find yourself in a highly stressful situation, your brain might start firing off warning signs, flashing lights, and go all "Mayday, Mayday!!!" on your ass. When this happens, your brain short circuits and goes straight to survival mode, which is all about the fight, flight, freeze, and fawn responses. These responses live in the amygdala, or the reptilian brain, as some people call it. It resides in the center/back part of your brain, kind of near your brain stem. The amygdala is all about keeping you alive so you can live another day, which is a job she (because, let's face it, it's the women in this world that keep people alive, so now we'll just refer to her as Amy) takes very seriously.

On the other hand, your critical thinking lives in your prefrontal cortex (PFC) which is located right behind your forehead. This is where you can think ahead, use math, problem solving skills, and communicate effectively. It's been shown that when Amy takes charge and goes into triage mode, she loses access to the PFC. This is why it's so difficult to think and act rationally while you're triggered and losing your shit. It's almost as if those obnoxiously dinging railroad crossing gates (you know, the ones that lower into the road so you don't get hit by a train?) show up in the middle of your brain, preventing you from getting away from Amy and into the PFC area. This is important when there's an actual threat in front of you because it forces you to divert all your energy into surviving, however, it's quite inconvenient when there's no actual threat.

For example, if you're walking in the woods and you stumble across a bear, Amy is going to take over and determine the best ways to survive this encounter. This is great news because I feel like no one actually wants to die by said bear. Which is also why you should always walk in the woods with a friend...IYKYK. Additionally, Amy is very smart and remembers everything you've ever gone through in your interesting little life. She gathers all the information and then applies it to current and future situations to help keep you safe. This is all well and dandy most days, but when she starts applying her extreme approaches to when there are no bears popping out of the woods, she can become a bit over bearing. (Get it? Bear. Over bearing. Sigh, don't worry, I won't quit my day job. *eye roll*) This is when your anxiety or other trauma responses start showing up when there's no actual threat in front of you. What is actually happening is that your body has a feeling, Amy identifies the feeling as a threat because she's felt it before in a threatening situation, applies it to the current event, and then takes over. She can be a bit of a bossy bitch though, so even though you know logically there's no bear, she doesn't give a fuck and applies what has worked in the past to the current situation. This is when you may start noticing how your anxiety and trauma are negatively impacting your life.

Also, the more Amy has had to work in your lifetime, such as chronic childhood trauma, unhealthy relationships, and an unstable home life, the bigger and bossier she gets as you get older. She becomes the helicopter parent you wish you never had as she sticks her nose into EVERYTHING you do. Then, at the slightest hint of discomfort, she swoops in and takes over instead of letting you breathe and process the situation on your own. She needs to feel needed and struggles with you becoming more independent so you can learn how to self soothe. What she doesn't realize, however, is how exhausted she actually is. As well as how much more efficient you could run your life once you learn how to sit with discomfort, be with your feelings productively, identify them, and apply some coping skills to help you get better. She just has to learn how to Let It Go! Let It GO!!!

Practicing these skills will also help that "in between time" get longer. You know, that space that is "in between" you feeling the feeling and reacting? Some people tell me that there is no space, there's just the event and then the reactions. They go from 0 to 60 real quick and don't remember what happened or how they even got there. Well, I hate to break it to you sweetheart, but there is, in fact, a space in between, but a lot of us weren't taught to pay attention to it. Some spaces are longer than other's because that human has had more practice with self-regulation. The goal is to work on identifying when your body is giving you the warning signals and then to practice a coping skill before you get to the point of no return. This may come easily for some, and more difficult for others, and that's ok. You are where you are, the question is, do you want to stay there or improve? No one can make you do anything, especially *want* to do something. (Parents understand this intrinsically. Have you ever tried to make your child WANT to clean their room? It didn't always work so great, did it?) This is purely an internal dialogue you get to have with yourself and decide which path you'd like to take. One of the best ways to get better at the "in between's" is to practice #8 on the coping skills list. That way you can work on identifying what exactly your body is telling you, instead of getting flooded and shutting down, which will also assist you with responding to the stressor instead of reacting to it.

Some of these coping skills may be obvious or generic to you because you've learned them before, and some might be new. Because some people numb out so much they don't know what they're feeling and others feel so much they don't know what they're feeling, practicing these coping skills will help you process your process. One other thing I've learned though, is no matter how silly or mundane they might feel, the important thing is that you actually put effort into them and try, otherwise nothing will work for you. Also, when I say "try", I don't mean half assing them while you're livid and then getting exasperated and think, "See! I knew this shit wouldn't work!". Naw, you're right, that's not how this shit works because that's self-defeating behavior that will keep you in a negative feedback loop and have you continuing on your own self destructive roller coaster. What I mean by "try", is practicing these skills not only while you're agitated, but also while you're calm. It's unfair to expect yourself to participate in a new behavior while you're already escalated, so that's why we practice these when we're bored or in a relaxed space. It helps create new neuro pathways and muscle memory for when you really do need them in your life.

So do your best to be open minded. Give them a chance, well hopefully a few chances, and see which ones resonate with you. These are here to help, so just keep swimming.

chapter 3

COPING SKILLS

Emotions list

Joy	Love	Surprise	Sadness
Enthralled	Peaceful	Stunned	Suffering
Elation	Tenderness	Confused	Sad
Enthusiastic	Desire	Amazed	Tearful
Optimistic	Longing	Overcome	Disappointed
Proud	Affectionate	Moved	Shameful
Cheerful	Satisfied	Shocked	Neglected
Happy	Relieved	Dismayed	Despair
Content	Compassionate	Disillusioned	Agony
Raptured	Caring	Perplexed	Hurt
Enchanted	Infatuation	Astonished	Depressed
Jubilation	Passion	Speechless	Sorrow
Euphoric	Attracted	Astounded	Displeased
Excited	Sentimental	Stimulated	Regretful
Hopeful	Fondness	Touched	Guilty
Eager	Romantic	Distracted	Isolated
Pleased	Thankful	Lonely	Grief
Satisfied	Balanced	**Fear**	Powerless
Amused	Trusting	Overwhelmed	Disconnected
Delighted	Relaxed	Nervous	Indifferent
Jovial	Insecure	Lazy	Defeated
Blissful	**Angry**	Terror	Embarrassed
Triumphant	Rage	Scared	Exhausted
Honored	Exasperated	Dread	Heartbroken
Creative	Irritable	Mortified	Longing
	Envious	Anxious	
	Disgusted	Worried	
	Revolted	Inadequate	
	Contempt	Inferior	
	Jealous	Hysterical	
	Resentful	Panic	
	Annoyed	Torn	
	Frustrated	Uneasy	
	Agitated	Guarded	
	Powerless	Conflicted	
	Defensive	Clingy	
	Grumpy	Vulnerable	
	Impatient	Helpless	
	Pessimistic	Suspicious	
	Self-Critical	Rejected	

1. Sit quietly. Look around you and notice:

- **5** things you can see: Your hands, the sky, a plant, your fur baby

- **4** things you can physically feel: Your feet on the ground, your hands running over the table or your legs, your friend's hand, your fur baby

- **3** things you can hear: The wind blowing, children's laughter, your breath, your fur baby barking or purring

- **2** things you can smell: Fresh-cut grass, coffee, soap, perfume, the cat litter, wet dog

- **1** thing you can taste: A mint, gum, the fresh air, skittles, chocolate, hair that's gotten in your mouth from said fur baby

This activity helps you get and remain grounded in the present moment despite what your racing thoughts are trying to accomplish.

2. Count by 7's or 8's until you get to at least 100. The goal is to stay in your prefrontal cortex so you don't slip into your survival brain, the amygdala. Counting by a weird number (yes, this is a technical term :P) will force you to focus on a very specific activity that requires a different part of your brain. So because your brain can't operate from your amygdala and your prefrontal cortex at the same time, it has to choose. This will help you stay calm so you can respond instead of react.

3. Name as many animals you can starting with a specific letter, then move on to a different one and so on. You can also name as many types of animals in a category, such as big cats or dog breeds. If for some reason you don't like animals, pick whichever topic you're interested in, such as cars, cooking utensils, stars, zodiac signs, bones, etc. If you'd like, you can set a timer for 1 minute, and then move on to the next option to give yourself a sense of urgency. This does the same thing to your brain as counting by 7's, just more fun.

4. 4 square breathing. You breathe in through your *nose* for 4 seconds, hold it for 4 seconds, breathe out through your *mouth* for 4 seconds, and then hold for 4 seconds. Do this at least 3 times in a row. You can also put your hand over your heart while doing this activity, this will help you feel more grounded and aware of your breathing. Breathing in through your nose and out through your mouth helps recalibrate your circulatory system and allows you to get back in your body. There are a few variations of this that are also helpful. See 5-7.

5. After practicing the 4 square breathing until you're comfortable, you might notice that you like breathing out longer than breathing in, or vice versa. Play around with what feels good. Each day might feel a little different, but I've noticed for me, breathing out longer feels better to really calm myself down and get centered. So sometimes it might be in for 4, hold for 5, out for 7, hold for 4 as an example. It might also help to scale (0-10) how anxious or pissed off you are before you do the breathing, and then afterwards. Then you can decide if you need to do another round of 3 breaths or if you'd like to stop.

6. Use Bubbles!!! I love bubbles. They're fun, silly, nostalgic, and cheap when you find the small pocket size ones on Amazon. Plus, how can you stay mad while blowing bubbles? So do the breathing as mentioned above in 4 and 5, but when you blow out, you are blowing bubbles. While the bubbles are around you, pick one bubble and watch it. Notice if it's a big or little bubble, high off the ground or low, moving fast or slow. Watch it until it goes poof. If there are still other bubbles around when it poofs, pick another one. Just sit with you and the bubbles until there are none left then repeat at least 2 more times.

7. Bubbles part 2. Try to see how big of a bubble you can blow. By doing this, you are concentrating on slowing down your breathing and solely focusing on the bubble at hand.

8. Use the Feelings list above, choose which emotion you identify most with at the moment. Being able to slow down and identify exactly what it is that you're feeling helps your body and brain connect. Sometimes we feel so much we don't know what we're feeling, while other times we numb out so much we don't know what we're feeling. Looking at the list of emotions can help us be more intentional with knowing how we're feeling instead of, "You know, just livin the dream" or "I'm fine, just tired".

- Scale the intensity of the emotion from 0-10. 0 being none at all and 10 being the fucking worst.

- Where are you feeling that emotion in your body? Do you notice it in your chest, head, hands, stomach?

- What physical sensations is that emotion causing within those body parts? Tightness, tingly, sharp, heavy, light, butterflies, cold, hot, jittery etc.

- If it had a shape, what would it be? (I know, weird af question, just go with it.)

- If it had a color, what would it be?

- Practice the breathing techniques from #4 or #5 while sitting in your feelings and noticing what is happening within your body.

- If you want to get creative, when you breathe in, imagine a golden light entering your nose and reaching every part of the inside of your body and soul, then when you breathe out, imagine those icky feelings you identified earlier leaving through your mouth. Imagine the light healing the disruptive sensations and then blowing out the darkness into the universe.

9. Refer to number 8, and when you're ready to do the breathing part, put your hand over your heart and repeat this script at least 3 times while taking a deep breath in between each repetition.

Thank you ___(Emotion)___ for protecting me,
and you are no longer needed.
I bless you. I honor you. It is safe to let you go now.

When you've done that 3 times, check back in with yourself. Where are you on your 0-10 scale? Is that emotion you originally targeted still the number one emotion you're feeling right now or is there a louder emotion that's sitting next to it? If it's still the original emotion and you're still a 5 or higher, do it at least 3 more times until it gets to a 1-3 on your scale or until you're at a number you're more comfortable with. If you notice a different emotion making itself known, rinse and repeat 8 and 9. Keep going until you feel at peace and you're able to think more clearly.

10. Ice Ice Baby! If you're currently in panic mode or just really anxious, go grab an ice pack or a bag of frozen vegetables from the freezer. (If you're trying to fall asleep, use the ice pack because we don't need you passing out and waking up with melting veggie juice all over you and your bed.) Then either sit or lay down in a quiet space, put the cold item directly on your chest or the back of your neck, and practice your 4 Square Breathing. Do this for at least 5 minutes. If it's too cold directly on your skin, you can use a shirt or towel as a barrier. The goal is for you to feel the bite of the cold though, so use your best judgement. What this does is stimulate your Vagus Nerve, restricts the blood vessels there, and tricks your mind and body into thinking it's more relaxed than it is. You can look more into this here: https://psychcentral.com/anxiety/vagus-nerve-cooling-anxiety#the-vagus-nerve if you'd like.

11. Scream. For real. Scream and let it the fuck out! Scream in your car, scream in your pillow, scream in the elevator at work or even in the walk in freezer (all you servers know what I'm talking about).

chapter 4

A " H O W   T O "   G U I D E

As you start reading through these questions, some of them might sound weird or unconventional to you, so I figured I'd provide some context ahead of time. First things first, we are all the ages we've ever been. Not only are you your current age, but you're also all the years you've lived previously, such as 24, 16, 10, 3, and so on. (Trust me, this is real. I have a very defiant 13yr old self living inside me and she's sassy AF.) You are built up of all the experiences you've ever been through because your cellular memory remembers everything you've ever experienced. You might not remember these things consciously, but your DNA has it memorized. If you'd like to take a more in depth look into cellular memory and how trauma effects the body, I would recommend The Body Keeps The Score by Dr. Van Der Kolk. This book will provide you a more in depth look at trauma, epigenetics, and why your body does the things it does.

So, for example, you're 25yrs old and you and your partner are arguing and it's getting pretty heated, then they end up calling you crazy or stupid and you lose your shit (Like in the movie, Hancock). Afterwards, you look back and ask yourself, "How did that set me off to that extreme?" Well, ask yourself this, "Did an adult ever called me crazy or stupid when I was little?". "Was I feeling crazy or stupid when I struggled with school or was I ashamed for not being good or smart enough?" Then move on to, "Was it really my 25yr old self acting that extreme or my 8 or 14 year old self that lost their shit?". That could be why the explosion was so intense, because when children have big feelings, everyone around them knows it. So the goal is to be curious and communicate with that younger version of yourself and see what messages they have for you. What they were trying to protect you from and how you can help them feel more safe?

With that being said, if one of the journaling questions asks about your little kid self, I want you to envision you as that little kid. What are you wearing? How old are you? What is your body language conveying? While answering the inner child questions, a different age might come to mind depending on the question. Just go with it. There are no wrong ways to answer them. Do your best not to over think and just start with your first instinct and keep diving deep. Follow the flow of thoughts and allow your intuition to guide you.

During this journaling process, you might find yourself getting defensive for either yourself or the caregivers in your life. During those lovely moments where excuses or rationalities might come into play regarding why a caregiver did or didn't do the things or why you should or shouldn't feel a certain way, just remember that "yabuts live in the woods". These are the wise words of my father, Steve. When we were little and he told us to do something we didn't want to do, we'd complain and say, "Yea, but...(enter excuse)" and then he'd reply with "Yabuts live in the woods". For those of you who still haven't gotten the joke, rabbits...yabuts. Get it now? (We're from Wisconsin, don't judge us and our pronunciations. We also rhyme milk with elk, so there's that. lol) It's the epitome of a dad joke and I never in a million years would have thought I would carry that phrase all the way into my therapy practice many years later. Also, when we use the word "but" instead of "and", it cancels out everything we said prior to it. It's like multiplying what we just communicated by zero. So when you start noticing yourself going "Yea, but they did the best they could", or "Yea, but I didn't know", or even, "Yea, but I don't know how to start". Just remember, those excuses do not belong on the healing journey because they live in the woods. The goal is to turn "yabuts" into "yea, ands". "YEA your caregivers did the best they could with what they had, AND it still wasn't what you needed growing up." "YEA you didn't know this would happen, AND now you do, so what can you do differently next time?" "YEA you may not know where to start, AND who can you go to for guidance?".

Next up on the list, writing options. Below are a few different examples that will provide some insight as to how in depth you may or may not want to go and how that could impact the usefulness of this activity. The levels of which you answer the questions might also change day by day depending on how much you resonate with a question or even how you're feeling emotionally that day. There's no wrong way to do it, except for not doing them at all.

Question: *When you expressed your emotions as a child, how were they received by the adults in your life? What did you learn from their reactions?*

Fluffy Answer: I wasn't really allowed to express any emotions that my parents didn't like. If I did, they'd get mad and tell me to stop or go to my room.

I'm Kinda Feelin' It Answer: Well, it depends on the kinds of emotions I expressed. If I was angry and started yelling, that would be a problem. They'd usually yell back until I either stopped or got dragged to my room for being disrespectful. I'd have to stay there for hours until they said I could come out, but even then they'd give me the cold shoulder. On the other hand, if I was happy, they'd be nicer around me because I wasn't embarrassing them.

Letting It All Hang Out Answer: It varied on which emotions I was expressing, but to be honest, if I wasn't doing it in the way they wanted me to, I got negative reactions from them no matter what. If I was mad or crying, they would meet my energy and start yelling back. I'd have to stop or they would physically drag me to my room until I "calmed down", but it was really when they actually remembered I was in there or dinner was ready. Sometimes they might even have spanked or hit me over the head if they felt like it. I never knew when that would happen though, and it was really confusing. They never talked to me about what happened afterwards, either. They usually just ignored me for a bit or acted like nothing occurred and expected me to "get over it". On the other hand, if my happy moods got too extra, they'd also scold me for being too demanding or loud. I would get harsh looks or get reprimanded so I'd stop being so obnoxious. I learned early on that when I was around them, I was only allowed to behave in generic and muted ways so I didn't disturb their emotions too much. I always vowed I would never treat my children like that if I had them. It was so fucked up.

So, silly question, but what do you notice about each one of these examples? How are they different and how are they the same? Can you see what I meant earlier about the fluffy level containing more safety and vagueness than the other two levels? None of these answers are correct or wrong, they're just different and contain a varying amount of information. Generally speaking, the more information you provide, the more you have to work with. It's ok that some answers might be more generic than others, or that some might contain more ugly stories, that's just how life works. Be patient with yourself and Hakuna Matata.

chapter 5

JOURNALING PROMPTS

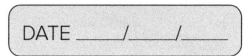

DATE _____ / _____ / _____

Emotion of the day_____

I'm grateful for_____

1. Day one or one day?

_____

_____

_____

_____

_____

_____

_____

_____

_____

_____

_____

_____

_____

_____

DATE _____ / _____ / _____

Emotion of the day _____

I'm grateful for _____

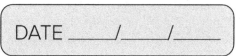

2. What does Shadow Work mean to me? What do I want to get out of this process?

_____

_____

_____

_____

_____

_____

_____

_____

_____

_____

_____

_____

DATE _____ / _____ / _____

Emotion of the day _____

I'm grateful for _____

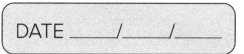

3. How will I know this journaling process has been useful? How will my life look different?

_____

_____

_____

_____

_____

_____

_____

_____

_____

_____

_____

_____

_____

DATE _____ / _____ / _____

Emotion of the day _____

I'm grateful for _____

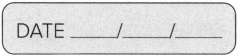

4. How did my parent's relationship set me up for success or failure? Is that something I've thought about often or is this the first time?

_____

_____

_____

_____

_____

_____

_____

_____

_____

_____

_____

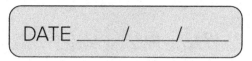

DATE ____ / ____ / ____

Emotion of the day _____

I'm grateful for _____

5. How were relationships modeled for me growing up? How did that impact my view on what a healthy relationship looks like?

_____

_____

_____

_____

_____

_____

_____

_____

_____

_____

_____

_____

_____

_____

_____

DATE _____ / _____ / _____

Emotion of the day _____

I'm grateful for _____

6. Who made me feel the best about myself growing up? How did they achieve that?

_____

_____

_____

_____

_____

_____

_____

_____

_____

_____

_____

_____

DATE _____/_____/_____

Emotion of the day_____

I'm grateful for_____

7. *Check In! What was journaling this week like for you? Where did you excel and where did you struggle? What new insights came up for you and how are you handling them? Which questions were more challenging than the others? Is there anything else that has happened this week that you'd like to sort through?*

_____

_____

_____

_____

_____

_____

_____

_____

_____

_____

DATE _____ / _____ / _____

Emotion of the day _____

I'm grateful for _____

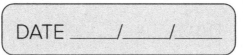

8. What was I brought up to value in my family? How are my current values similar or different?

_____

_____

_____

_____

_____

_____

_____

_____

_____

_____

_____

_____

_____

DATE ____ / ____ / ____

Emotion of the day _____

I'm grateful for _____

9. What did I see as a child that I don't want to duplicate as an adult? How come?

_____

_____

_____

_____

_____

_____

_____

_____

_____

_____

_____

_____

_____

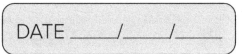

DATE _____/_____/_____

Emotion of the day_____

I'm grateful for_____

10. How have some of my fears kept me safe in the past? How do they still serve me? Which, if any, can I let go of?

_____

_____

_____

_____

_____

_____

_____

_____

_____

_____

_____

_____

_____

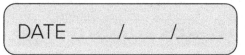

DATE _____/_____/_____

Emotion of the day_____

I'm grateful for_____

11. What would have helped me feel more safe (emotionally or physically) growing up? What or who prevented me from receiving it?

_____

_____

_____

_____

_____

_____

_____

_____

_____

_____

_____

DATE _____/_____/_____

Emotion of the day _____

I'm grateful for _____

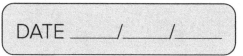

12. How have I managed to survive the traumas I've experienced? In what ways did I feel in and out of control during that process?

_____

_____

_____

_____

_____

_____

_____

_____

_____

_____

_____

Emotion of the day_____

I'm grateful for_____

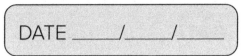

13. If I loved myself, how would I live my life differently? What would my world look like?

_____

_____

_____

_____

_____

_____

_____

_____

_____

_____

_____

_____

DATE _____ / _____ / _____

Emotion of the day _____

I'm grateful for _____

14. *Check In! What was journaling this week like for you? Where did you excel and where did you struggle? What new insights came up for you and how are you handling them? Which questions were more challenging than the others? Is there anything else that has happened this week that you'd like to sort through?*

_____

_____

_____

_____

_____

_____

_____

_____

_____

_____

_____

DATE _____/_____/_____

Emotion of the day_____

I'm grateful for_____

15. In the past, where have I tried to fix things for other people when it wasn't my responsibility to fix them? Do I feel certain people have needed me to step in more than others?

_____

_____

_____

_____

_____

_____

_____

_____

_____

_____

DATE _____ / _____ / _____

Emotion of the day _____

I'm grateful for _____

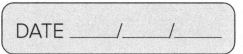

16. Looking at the current challenges in my life, which ones are mine and which ones am I taking responsibility for even though they belong to other people? What would happen if I gave that responsibility back to the person it belonged to?

_____

_____

_____

_____

_____

_____

_____

_____

_____

_____

_____

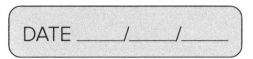

DATE _____/_____/_____

Emotion of the day_____

I'm grateful for_____

17. What are some of the limiting beliefs I learned as a child that have held me back in life? Who taught them to me and how have they kept me safe?

_____

_____

_____

_____

_____

_____

_____

_____

_____

_____

_____

_____

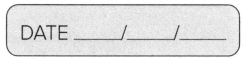

DATE ____/____/____

Emotion of the day_____

I'm grateful for_____

18. Was I allowed to say "No" or ask "Why?" growing up? How was that received in my family if I did? How has this affected me as an adult?

_____

_____

_____

_____

_____

_____

_____

_____

_____

_____

_____

DATE _____/_____/_____

Emotion of the day_____

I'm grateful for_____

☼   ☁   ⚡   🌈   ❄

19. Who taught me to put their needs before my own? If no one, who taught me to value my emotional needs first?

_____

_____

_____

_____

_____

_____

_____

_____

_____

_____

_____

_____

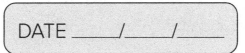

DATE _____/_____/_____

Emotion of the day_____

I'm grateful for_____

20. Did my caregivers provide me with support even if I wasn't successful in something? Elaborate.

_____

_____

_____

_____

_____

_____

_____

_____

_____

_____

_____

_____

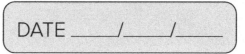

DATE _____/_____/_____

Emotion of the day_____

I'm grateful for_____

21. *Check In! What was journaling this week like for you? Where did you excel and where did you struggle? What new insights came up for you and how are you handling them? Which questions were more challenging than the others? Is there anything else that has happened this week that you'd like to sort through?*

_____

_____

_____

_____

_____

_____

_____

_____

_____

_____

_____

DATE ____/____/____

Emotion of the day_____

I'm grateful for_____

22. When was the last time I forgave myself for doing something I wished I didn't? What do I still need to forgive myself for?

_____

_____

_____

_____

_____

_____

_____

_____

_____

_____

_____

_____

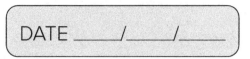

DATE _____ / _____ / _____

Emotion of the day_____

I'm grateful for_____

23. What past version of myself do I hope no one ever sees and why? Who taught me to hide?

_____

_____

_____

_____

_____

_____

_____

_____

_____

_____

_____

_____

DATE _____/_____/_____

Emotion of the day_____

I'm grateful for_____

24. In what areas in my life have I struggled to forgive myself? What prevents me from letting it go?

_____

_____

_____

_____

_____

_____

_____

_____

_____

_____

_____

_____

DATE ____/____/____

Emotion of the day_____

I'm grateful for_____

25. What has been my biggest personal failure and why do I think it's a failure? Would other people consider it that way?

_____

_____

_____

_____

_____

_____

_____

_____

_____

_____

_____

_____

DATE ____/____/____

Emotion of the day_____

I'm grateful for_____

26. Growing up, who taught me how to love? What was considered loving in my family?

_____

_____

_____

_____

_____

_____

_____

_____

_____

_____

_____

_____

_____

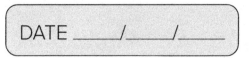

DATE ____/____/____

Emotion of the day_____

I'm grateful for_____

27. *Check In! What was journaling this week like for you? Where did you excel and where did you struggle? What new insights came up for you and how are you handling them? Which questions were more challenging than the others? Is there anything else that has happened this week that you'd like to sort through?*

_____

_____

_____

_____

_____

_____

_____

_____

_____

_____

_____

DATE _____/_____/_____

Emotion of the day _____

I'm grateful for _____

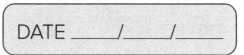

28. How was I taught to process my emotions as a child? As a teenager?

_____

_____

_____

_____

_____

_____

_____

_____

_____

_____

_____

_____

Emotion of the day_____

I'm grateful for_____

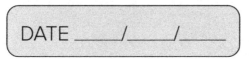

29. When I expressed my emotions as a child, how were they received by the adults in my life? What did I learn from their reactions?

_____

_____

_____

_____

_____

_____

_____

_____

_____

_____

_____

_____

DATE _____ / _____ / _____

Emotion of the day_____

I'm grateful for_____

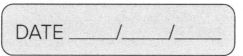

30. What was a quality that I had as a child that I liked? Do I still retain that quality? If no, do I wish I did and if yes, how has it grown?

_____

_____

_____

_____

_____

_____

_____

_____

_____

_____

_____

_____

DATE ____/____/____

Emotion of the day_____

I'm grateful for_____

31. If I could change one thing in my family growing up, what would it have been and why?

_____

_____

_____

_____

_____

_____

_____

_____

_____

_____

_____

_____

_____

Emotion of the day_____

I'm grateful for_____

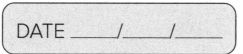

32. Who hurt me the most during my childhood? What was my relationship like with them compared to now?

_____

_____

_____

_____

_____

_____

_____

_____

_____

_____

_____

_____

DATE _____ / _____ / _____

Emotion of the day _____

I'm grateful for _____

33. As a child, was I allowed to place boundaries with the adults in my life? If so, what were the boundaries? How did I learn and what would happen if I didn't abide by them?

_____

_____

_____

_____

_____

_____

_____

_____

_____

_____

_____

DATE _____ / _____ / _____

Emotion of the day_____

I'm grateful for_____

34. As a child, what would happen if I expressed anger or displeasure to my caregiver? How do I feel about expressing my anger now?

_____

_____

_____

_____

_____

_____

_____

_____

_____

_____

_____

DATE _____ / _____ / _____

Emotion of the day _____

I'm grateful for _____

35. *Check In! What was journaling this week like for you? Where did you excel and where did you struggle? What new insights came up for you and how are you handling them? Which questions were more challenging than the others? Is there anything else that has happened this week that you'd like to sort through?*

_____

_____

_____

_____

_____

_____

_____

_____

_____

_____

_____

DATE _____ / _____ / _____

Emotion of the day _____

I'm grateful for _____

36. What could I have told my little kid self that would have instilled hope for the future? Does that same wisdom apply to me today?

_____

_____

_____

_____

_____

_____

_____

_____

_____

_____

_____

_____

DATE _____ / _____ / _____

Emotion of the day _____

I'm grateful for _____

37. As a child, who was my hero and why did I look up to them? If I'd known then what I know now, would they still be my hero?

_____

_____

_____

_____

_____

_____

_____

_____

_____

_____

_____

_____

DATE _____ / _____ / _____

Emotion of the day _____

I'm grateful for _____

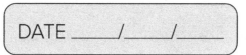

38. How have I overcame one of my fears? What strengths and skills did it take for me to do that?

_____

_____

_____

_____

_____

_____

_____

_____

_____

_____

_____

_____

DATE ____/____/____

Emotion of the day_____

I'm grateful for_____

39. What was I not allowed to do, but other children could, growing up.

_____
_____
_____
_____
_____
_____
_____
_____
_____
_____
_____
_____

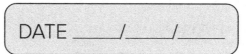

DATE _____ / _____ / _____

Emotion of the day _____

I'm grateful for _____

40. Who helped me survive my childhood? What kind of relation-ship do I currently have with them?

_____

_____

_____

_____

_____

_____

_____

_____

_____

_____

_____

_____

DATE _____ / _____ / _____

Emotion of the day _____

I'm grateful for _____

41. What did I need most as a child that I didn't receive? How can I provide that for my inner child now?

_____

_____

_____

_____

_____

_____

_____

_____

_____

_____

_____

_____

_____

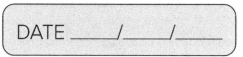

DATE _____/_____/_____

Emotion of the day_____

I'm grateful for_____

42. *Check In! What was journaling this week like for you? Where did you excel and where did you struggle? What new insights came up for you and how are you handling them? Which questions were more challenging than the others? Is there anything else that has happened this week that you'd like to sort through?*

_____

_____

_____

_____

_____

_____

_____

_____

_____

_____

DATE _____/_____/_____

Emotion of the day_____

I'm grateful for_____

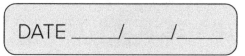

43. Where was I in the sibling line up? How did that impact the relationships I had with my parents and siblings? If I'm an only child, what was that like?

_____

_____

_____

_____

_____

_____

_____

_____

_____

_____

_____

DATE _____/_____/_____

Emotion of the day_____

I'm grateful for_____

44. What role did I play in my family growing up? How have I inte-
grated that role into my current relationships?

_____

_____

_____

_____

_____

_____

_____

_____

_____

_____

_____

_____

_____

DATE _____/_____/_____

Emotion of the day_____

I'm grateful for_____

45. What were some similarities and differences in the relationships my parents had with me versus my siblings? If I'm an only child, what did I notice was different between the relationship I had with my parents versus my friends that had siblings?

_____

_____

_____

_____

_____

_____

_____

_____

_____

_____

_____

_____

DATE ____/____/____

Emotion of the day_____

I'm grateful for_____

46. If I were my parent as a child, what would I have done differently? What would I have done the same?

_____

_____

_____

_____

_____

_____

_____

_____

_____

_____

_____

_____

_____

DATE _____ / _____ / _____

Emotion of the day _____

I'm grateful for _____

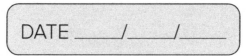

47. What advantages or disadvantages did I have being the only/youngest/middle/oldest child? Do I have any strong feelings regarding the way any of my siblings were treated compared to myself?

_____

_____

_____

_____

_____

_____

_____

_____

_____

_____

_____

_____

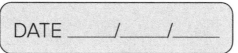

DATE _____/_____/_____

Emotion of the day_____

I'm grateful for_____

48. Is there anything my teenage self is still angry about? How can I comfort them now?

_____

_____

_____

_____

_____

_____

_____

_____

_____

_____

_____

_____

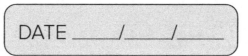

DATE _____/_____/_____

Emotion of the day_____

I'm grateful for_____

49. *Check In! What was journaling this week like for you? Where did you excel and where did you struggle? What new insights came up for you and how are you handling them? Which questions were more challenging than the others? Is there anything else that has happened this week that you'd like to sort through?*

_____

_____

_____

_____

_____

_____

_____

_____

_____

_____

DATE ____/____/____

Emotion of the day _____

I'm grateful for _____

50. Looking at my past, who has a history of downplaying how I truly felt? Does anyone in my life currently do that? How do I respond to those people now, compared to how I did as a child?

_____

_____

_____

_____

_____

_____

_____

_____

_____

_____

_____

DATE _____ / _____ / _____

Emotion of the day _____

I'm grateful for _____

51. What events in my life have hurt me the most? What reminds me of these times? What parts of me remain in those memories?

_____
_____
_____
_____
_____
_____
_____
_____
_____
_____
_____
_____
_____

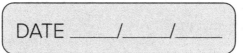

DATE _____/_____/_____

Emotion of the day_____

I'm grateful for_____

52. When have I opened up to someone and felt rejected? What did I share and how did they respond?

_____

_____

_____

_____

_____

_____

_____

_____

_____

_____

_____

_____

DATE _____/_____/_____

Emotion of the day_____

I'm grateful for_____

53. When was the last time I felt defensive and who or what caused that feeling? How did I respond/react to it? How could I have handled it better?

_____

_____

_____

_____

_____

_____

_____

_____

_____

_____

_____

DATE _____ / _____ / _____

Emotion of the day_____

I'm grateful for_____

54. What were the similarities and differences between how my teenage and younger childhood selves handled stress?

_____

_____

_____

_____

_____

_____

_____

_____

_____

_____

_____

_____

DATE _____ / _____ / _____

Emotion of the day_____

I'm grateful for_____

55. Looking back to my teenage years, what are some things I accomplished that still makes me proud today? What did I have to overcome in order to achieve those triumphs?

_____

_____

_____

_____

_____

_____

_____

_____

_____

_____

_____

_____

DATE _____/_____/_____

Emotion of the day_____

I'm grateful for_____

56. *Check In! What was journaling this week like for you? Where did you excel and where did you struggle? What new insights came up for you and how are you handling them? Which questions were more challenging than the others? Is there anything else that has happened this week that you'd like to sort through?*

_____

_____

_____

_____

_____

_____

_____

_____

_____

_____

DATE _____/_____/_____

Emotion of the day_____

I'm grateful for_____

57. In what ways am I like and not like my parents? How do I feel about these character traits?

_____

_____

_____

_____

_____

_____

_____

_____

_____

_____

_____

_____

_____

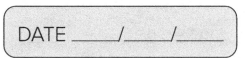

DATE _____/_____/_____

Emotion of the day_____

I'm grateful for_____

58. What family patterns do I fear I'm repeating? How can I acknowledge these patterns and what can I start doing differently to change them?

_____

_____

_____

_____

_____

_____

_____

_____

_____

_____

_____

DATE _____/_____/_____

Emotion of the day _____

I'm grateful for _____

59. How important were grades in my family? What happened if I received "good" grades? What about the "bad" ones?

_____

_____

_____

_____

_____

_____

_____

_____

_____

_____

_____

_____

_____

DATE _____ / _____ / _____

Emotion of the day_____

I'm grateful for_____

60. How did I gain respect growing up? How did I show respect to others? What does being respectful mean to me?

_____

_____

_____

_____

_____

_____

_____

_____

_____

_____

_____

_____

_____

DATE _____ / _____ / _____

Emotion of the day_____

I'm grateful for_____

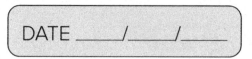

61. What was my relationship with my father like growing up? How has that impacted my relationship with men as I've gotten older?

_____

_____

_____

_____

_____

_____

_____

_____

_____

_____

_____

_____

_____

DATE _____ / _____ / _____

Emotion of the day _____

I'm grateful for _____

62. What was my relationship with my mother like growing up? How has that impacted my relationship with women as I've gotten older?

_____

_____

_____

_____

_____

_____

_____

_____

_____

_____

_____

_____

DATE _____ / _____ / _____

Emotion of the day_____

I'm grateful for_____

☀ ☁ ⛈ 🌈 🌨

63. *Check In! What was journaling this week like for you? Where did you excel and where did you struggle? What new insights came up for you and how are you handling them? Which questions were more challenging than the others? Is there anything else that has happened this week that you'd like to sort through?*

_____

_____

_____

_____

_____

_____

_____

_____

_____

_____

DATE _____/_____/_____

Emotion of the day _____

I'm grateful for _____

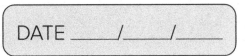

64. Write about a time when I had a positive impact on someone's life. How do I know it was positive? What's it like for me while writing about it?

_____

_____

_____

_____

_____

_____

_____

_____

_____

_____

_____

DATE _____ / _____ / _____

Emotion of the day _____

I'm grateful for _____

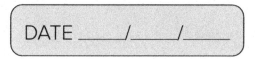

65. Put your hand over your heart, take a deep breath through your nose and out through your mouth and say, " I respect, I honor, and I love myself." What was that like for you? What emotions are you feeling?

_____

_____

_____

_____

_____

_____

_____

_____

_____

_____

_____

_____

DATE _____ / _____ / _____

Emotion of the day_____

I'm grateful for_____

66. What does it mean to love myself? What does loving myself look like, feel like, and sound like?

_____

_____

_____

_____

_____

_____

_____

_____

_____

_____

_____

_____

DATE ____ / ____ / ____

Emotion of the day _____

I'm grateful for _____

67. What is the biggest obstacle to finding the happiness that I crave? Who put that obstacle there? How can I start to make it smaller?

_____

_____

_____

_____

_____

_____

_____

_____

_____

_____

_____

DATE _____ / _____ / _____

Emotion of the day _____

I'm grateful for _____

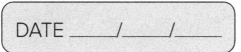

68. What is my definition of perfection? Is it attainable? Who taught me this mindset?

_____

_____

_____

_____

_____

_____

_____

_____

_____

_____

_____

_____

_____

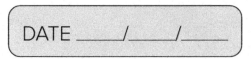

DATE _____/_____/_____

Emotion of the day_____

I'm grateful for_____

69. What does compassion mean to me? How can I show more compassion to myself? To others?

_____

_____

_____

_____

_____

_____

_____

_____

_____

_____

_____

_____

_____

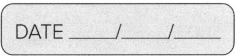

DATE _____/_____/_____

Emotion of the day_____

I'm grateful for_____

70. *Check In! What was journaling this week like for you? Where did you excel and where did you struggle? What new insights came up for you and how are you handling them? Which questions were more challenging than the others? Is there anything else that has happened this week that you'd like to sort through?*

_____

_____

_____

_____

_____

_____

_____

_____

_____

_____

DATE _____/_____/_____

Emotion of the day _____

I'm grateful for _____

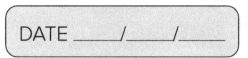

71. When was the first and last time I felt taken advantage of? How are they similar and different?

_____

_____

_____

_____

_____

_____

_____

_____

_____

_____

_____

_____

DATE _____ / _____ / _____

Emotion of the day _____

I'm grateful for _____

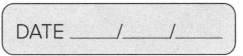

72. At what age did I first feel rejection? What happened? While thinking about that moment, where do I feel the rejection in my body and what sensations does it bring?

_____

_____

_____

_____

_____

_____

_____

_____

_____

_____

_____

_____

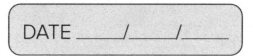

DATE ____ / ____ / ____

Emotion of the day_____

I'm grateful for_____

73. What methods did my caregivers use to get me to do the things they wanted? What happened if I didn't listen to them?

_____

_____

_____

_____

_____

_____

_____

_____

_____

_____

_____

_____

_____

DATE ____ / ____ / ____

Emotion of the day_____

I'm grateful for_____

74. What painful experience from my past do I feel still holds me back from further growth? How long have I been holding on to that experience?

_____

_____

_____

_____

_____

_____

_____

_____

_____

_____

_____

_____

DATE _____ / _____ / _____

Emotion of the day _____

I'm grateful for _____

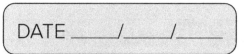

75. What did I do well in my childhood? How was I able to influence difficult situations to make them less harmful?

_____

_____

_____

_____

_____

_____

_____

_____

_____

_____

_____

_____

Emotion of the day_____

I'm grateful for_____

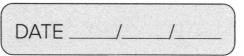

76. Who's needs came first in the home growing up and what would happen if their needs weren't met?

_____

_____

_____

_____

_____

_____

_____

_____

_____

_____

_____

_____

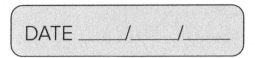

DATE ___/___/___

Emotion of the day_____

I'm grateful for_____

77. *Check In! What was journaling this week like for you? Where did you excel and where did you struggle? What new insights came up for you and how are you handling them? Which questions were more challenging than the others? Is there anything else that has happened this week that you'd like to sort through?*

_____

_____

_____

_____

_____

_____

_____

_____

_____

_____

DATE _____ / _____ / _____

Emotion of the day _____

I'm grateful for _____

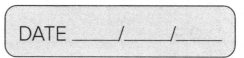

78. What did I worry about the most as a child? What about as a teenager?

_____

_____

_____

_____

_____

_____

_____

_____

_____

_____

_____

_____

_____

DATE _____ / _____ / _____

Emotion of the day _____

I'm grateful for _____

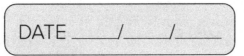

79. Was I ever bullied in school or was I ever the bully? What was that like for me?

_____

_____

_____

_____

_____

_____

_____

_____

_____

_____

_____

_____

DATE _____/_____/_____

Emotion of the day_____

I'm grateful for_____

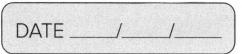

80. When did I feel like I couldn't stand up for myself at school or at home? What happens in my body while reliving that moment?

_____

_____

_____

_____

_____

_____

_____

_____

_____

_____

_____

_____

DATE _____ / _____ / _____

Emotion of the day _____

I'm grateful for _____

81. What helped me feel better when I was scared or sad as a child? Do I still participate in those activities?

_____

_____

_____

_____

_____

_____

_____

_____

_____

_____

_____

_____

_____

DATE _____ / _____ / _____

Emotion of the day _____

I'm grateful for _____

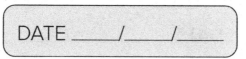

82. Do I feel anyone has ever been a bad friend to me? What happened and are we still friends today?

_____

_____

_____

_____

_____

_____

_____

_____

_____

_____

_____

_____

DATE _____/_____/_____

Emotion of the day_____

I'm grateful for_____

83. What did/does it mean to be popular in school? What do I think true popularity looks like? Do I think the popular kids went through the same challenges I did growing up?

_____

_____

_____

_____

_____

_____

_____

_____

_____

_____

_____

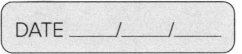

DATE _____/_____/_____

Emotion of the day _____

I'm grateful for _____

84. *Check In! What was journaling this week like for you? Where did you excel and where did you struggle? What new insights came up for you and how are you handling them? Which questions were more challenging than the others? Is there anything else that has happened this week that you'd like to sort through?*

_____

_____

_____

_____

_____

_____

_____

_____

_____

_____

DATE _____ / _____ / _____

Emotion of the day_____

I'm grateful for_____

85. Who taught me about sex growing up? How did the conversation go and looking back on that now, how would I have done it differently?

_____

_____

_____

_____

_____

_____

_____

_____

_____

_____

_____

_____

DATE _____/_____/_____

Emotion of the day_____

I'm grateful for_____

86. How did my family handle discussions about sex and intimacy? What could have gone better?

_____

_____

_____

_____

_____

_____

_____

_____

_____

_____

_____

_____

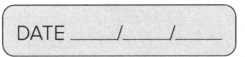

DATE ____/____/____

Emotion of the day_____

I'm grateful for_____

87. What was my first intimate experience like? How did that shape my views on sex?

_____

_____

_____

_____

_____

_____

_____

_____

_____

_____

_____

_____

_____

DATE _____/_____/_____

Emotion of the day_____

I'm grateful for_____

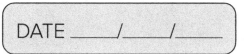

88. Have I ever been in a situation with a partner where I felt I couldn't say no to being intimate? What happened and how do I feel about the situation now?

_____

_____

_____

_____

_____

_____

_____

_____

_____

_____

_____

DATE ____/____/____

Emotion of the day _____

I'm grateful for _____

89. How old was I when I first experienced a healthy, loving relationship (either romantic or platonic)? Who was it with and what do I
remember most about them?

_____

_____

_____

_____

_____

_____

_____

_____

_____

_____

_____

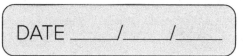

DATE _____ / _____ / _____

Emotion of the day _____

I'm grateful for _____

90. Who was the first person to break my heart? What happened and how does it still affect me?

_____

_____

_____

_____

_____

_____

_____

_____

_____

_____

_____

_____

DATE _____ / _____ / _____

Emotion of the day _____

I'm grateful for _____

91. *Check In! What was journaling this week like for you? Where did you excel and where did you struggle? What new insights came up for you and how are you handling them? Which questions were more challenging than the others? Is there anything else that has happened this week that you'd like to sort through?*

_____

_____

_____

_____

_____

_____

_____

_____

_____

_____

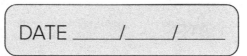

DATE _____ / _____ / _____

Emotion of the day_____

I'm grateful for_____

92. Who are the people that helped improve my life growing up? How do I know they helped?

_____

_____

_____

_____

_____

_____

_____

_____

_____

_____

_____

_____

DATE _____/_____/_____

Emotion of the day_____

I'm grateful for_____

93. When have I felt both relieved and devastated at the same time?

_____

_____

_____

_____

_____

_____

_____

_____

_____

_____

_____

_____

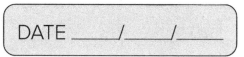

DATE ___/___/___

Emotion of the day _____

I'm grateful for _____

94. When has a fear of failure held myself back from an opportunity to grow? What have I learned from that?

_____

_____

_____

_____

_____

_____

_____

_____

_____

_____

_____

_____

_____

DATE _____/_____/_____

Emotion of the day_____

I'm grateful for_____

95. What achievement am I most proud of accomplishing? What skills did it take to accomplish that goal?

_____

_____

_____

_____

_____

_____

_____

_____

_____

_____

_____

_____

_____

DATE _____ / _____ / _____

Emotion of the day _____

I'm grateful for _____

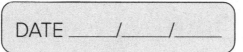

96. How Important am I to myself? Has anyone taught me that it's ok to prioritize my needs? Explain.

_____

_____

_____

_____

_____

_____

_____

_____

_____

_____

_____

_____

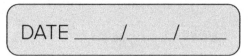

DATE _____ / _____ / _____

Emotion of the day_____

I'm grateful for_____

97. Where did I learn to choose violence/deflection/denial instead of vulnerability? In what ways has that served me?

_____

_____

_____

_____

_____

_____

_____

_____

_____

_____

_____

_____

_____

DATE _____/_____/_____

Emotion of the day_____

I'm grateful for_____

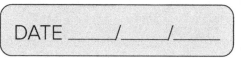

98. Check In! What was journaling this week like for you? Where did you excel and where did you struggle? What new insights came up for you and how are you handling them? Which questions were more challenging than the others? Is there anything else that has happened this week that you'd like to sort through?

_____

_____

_____

_____

_____

_____

_____

_____

_____

_____

DATE _____/_____/_____

Emotion of the day_____

I'm grateful for_____

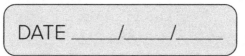

99. What activities did I do for fun as a child? Why did I stop participating in these activities? Would I like to resume them? Why or why not?

_____

_____

_____

_____

_____

_____

_____

_____

_____

_____

_____

_____

Emotion of the day_____

I'm grateful for_____

100. How old was I when I first felt guilty? What happened and how are my feelings towards that situation now?

_____

_____

_____

_____

_____

_____

_____

_____

_____

_____

_____

_____

_____

DATE _____/_____/_____

Emotion of the day _____

I'm grateful for _____

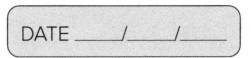

101. What does "Toxic Positivity" mean to me? Where do I notice this most in my life? When have I disregarded my real feelings in favor of "looking on the bright side"?

_____

_____

_____

_____

_____

_____

_____

_____

_____

_____

_____

_____

_____

DATE _____/_____/_____

Emotion of the day_____

I'm grateful for_____

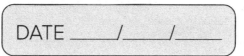

102. What's the biggest promise I've broken to myself? What happened and have I forgiven myself yet?

_____

_____

_____

_____

_____

_____

_____

_____

_____

_____

_____

_____

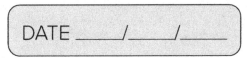

DATE ____/____/____

Emotion of the day_____

I'm grateful for_____

103. What were some of my strengths as a child? What about as a teenager? How did I develop these traits?

_____

_____

_____

_____

_____

_____

_____

_____

_____

_____

_____

_____

DATE ____/____/____

Emotion of the day———————————————————

I'm grateful for———————————————————

104. How did I express myself as a teenager? How was that accepted within my family unit?

_____

_____

_____

_____

_____

_____

_____

_____

_____

_____

_____

_____

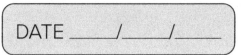

DATE _____ / _____ / _____

Emotion of the day _____

I'm grateful for _____

105. *Check In! What was journaling this week like for you? Where did you excel and where did you struggle? What new insights came up for you and how are you handling them? Which questions were more challenging than the others? Is there anything else that has happened this week that you'd like to sort through?*

_____

_____

_____

_____

_____

_____

_____

_____

_____

_____

_____

DATE _____/_____/_____

Emotion of the day _____

I'm grateful for _____

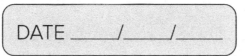

106. When was the last time I felt betrayed by someone? What happened and how did I respond? When was the first time I felt betrayed? Are there any similarities or differences?

_____

_____

_____

_____

_____

_____

_____

_____

_____

_____

_____

_____

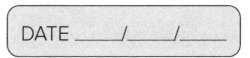

DATE ____ / ____ / ____

Emotion of the day _____

I'm grateful for _____

107. Who did I look up to growing up? Do I feel like my current self has similar qualities and characteristics as they did?

_____

_____

_____

_____

_____

_____

_____

_____

_____

_____

_____

_____

_____

DATE _____ / _____ / _____

Emotion of the day_____

I'm grateful for_____

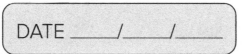

108. What relationship pattern has followed me throughout my life? What would happen if I broke this pattern?

_____

_____

_____

_____

_____

_____

_____

_____

_____

_____

_____

_____

DATE _____ / _____ / _____

Emotion of the day _____

I'm grateful for _____

109. How does anger function in my life? Do I have a healthy or unhealthy relationship with it?

_____

_____

_____

_____

_____

_____

_____

_____

_____

_____

_____

_____

_____

DATE _____/_____/_____

Emotion of the day_____

I'm grateful for_____

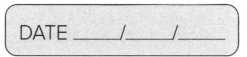

110. What negative emotions am I most comfortable with? Which emotions do I cling to on a day to day basis because they feel "normal"?

_____

_____

_____

_____

_____

_____

_____

_____

_____

_____

_____

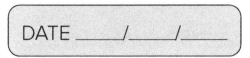

DATE _____/_____/_____

Emotion of the day_____

I'm grateful for_____

111. In what ways do I self-soothe? How functional are these methods? In what ways can I become more efficient at self-soothing?

_____

_____

_____

_____

_____

_____

_____

_____

_____

_____

_____

_____

DATE ____/____/____

Emotion of the day _____

I'm grateful for _____

112. *Check In! What was journaling this week like for you? Where did you excel and where did you struggle? What new insights came up for you and how are you handling them? Which questions were more challenging than the others? Is there anything else that has happened this week that you'd like to sort through?*

_____

_____

_____

_____

_____

_____

_____

_____

_____

_____

DATE ____/____/____

Emotion of the day_____

I'm grateful for_____

113. How can I be more kind to myself?

_____

_____

_____

_____

_____

_____

_____

_____

_____

_____

_____

_____

_____

DATE _____/_____/_____

Emotion of the day _____

I'm grateful for _____

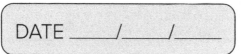

114. What is my relationship like with money and finances? How is this similar or different than what I saw growing up?

_____

_____

_____

_____

_____

_____

_____

_____

_____

_____

_____

_____

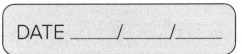

DATE ___/___/___

Emotion of the day_____

I'm grateful for_____

115. What does success look, sound, and feel like to me? If I achieved that success, would I still feel the way I do about my life right now?

_____

_____

_____

_____

_____

_____

_____

_____

_____

_____

_____

DATE _____ / _____ / _____

Emotion of the day_____

I'm grateful for_____

116. What are the differences and similarities between how I enforced boundaries as a child versus an adult?

_____

_____

_____

_____

_____

_____

_____

_____

_____

_____

_____

_____

DATE ____/____/____

Emotion of the day_____

I'm grateful for_____

117. Which emotions do I tend to avoid? How do I avoid them and what would happen if I let myself feel them?

_____
_____
_____
_____
_____
_____
_____
_____
_____
_____
_____
_____

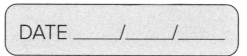

DATE _____/_____/_____

Emotion of the day_____

I'm grateful for_____

118. What is my relationship with alcohol and other substances like? How have they helped or caused challenges in my relationships?

_____

_____

_____

_____

_____

_____

_____

_____

_____

_____

_____

_____

_____

DATE _____ / _____ / _____

Emotion of the day _____

I'm grateful for _____

119. *Check In! What was journaling this week like for you? Where did you excel and where did you struggle? What new insights came up for you and how are you handling them? Which questions were more challenging than the others? Is there anything else that has happened this week that you'd like to sort through?*

_____

_____

_____

_____

_____

_____

_____

_____

_____

_____

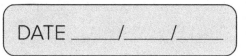

DATE _____/_____/_____

Emotion of the day_____

I'm grateful for_____

120. Who was my first love? How did this love impact my relationships later in life?

_____

_____

_____

_____

_____

_____

_____

_____

_____

_____

_____

_____

DATE ____/____/____

Emotion of the day_____

I'm grateful for_____

121. What's the biggest promise I've broken to myself? What happened and have I forgiven myself yet?

_____

_____

_____

_____

_____

_____

_____

_____

_____

_____

_____

_____

_____

_____

DATE ____ / ____ / ____

Emotion of the day _____

I'm grateful for _____

122. What is the most hurtful thing I have done to myself and what influenced my decision? How can I start healing that wound?

_____

_____

_____

_____

_____

_____

_____

_____

_____

_____

_____

_____

DATE _____ / _____ / _____

Emotion of the day _____

I'm grateful for _____

123. What does healthy love look/feel/sound like to me? How do I know it's healthy and where did I learn it from?

_____

_____

_____

_____

_____

_____

_____

_____

_____

_____

_____

_____

_____

DATE ____/____/____

Emotion of the day_____

I'm grateful for_____

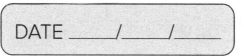

124. What aspects of my personality change when I'm single versus in a relationship?

_____

_____

_____

_____

_____

_____

_____

_____

_____

_____

_____

_____

DATE ____/____/____

Emotion of the day_____

I'm grateful for_____

125. What is one trait I see in other people that I wish I had? Why do I feel I don't possess this characteristic in myself? What actions can I take to start working towards gaining this trait?

_____

_____

_____

_____

_____

_____

_____

_____

_____

_____

_____

_____

DATE ____ / ____ / ____

Emotion of the day_____

I'm grateful for_____

126. *Check In! What was journaling this week like for you? Where did you excel and where did you struggle? What new insights came up for you and how are you handling them? Which questions were more challenging than the others? Is there anything else that has happened this week that you'd like to sort through?*

_____

_____

_____

_____

_____

_____

_____

_____

_____

_____

DATE _____ / _____ / _____

Emotion of the day _____

I'm grateful for _____

127. How do I feel about myself as a human? Would I choose to be friends with me?

_____

_____

_____

_____

_____

_____

_____

_____

_____

_____

_____

_____

DATE ____/____/____

Emotion of the day_____

I'm grateful for_____

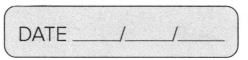

128. How often do I forgive myself? Are certain things easier to forgive than others? Which ones and why?

_____

_____

_____

_____

_____

_____

_____

_____

_____

_____

_____

_____

_____

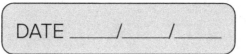

DATE _____ / _____ / _____

Emotion of the day_____

I'm grateful for_____

129. How can I learn to listen first before reacting? Which parts of me struggle with reacting instead of responding?

_____

_____

_____

_____

_____

_____

_____

_____

_____

_____

_____

_____

_____

DATE _____ / _____ / _____

Emotion of the day_____

I'm grateful for_____

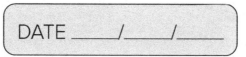

130. Are there any self-esteem issues holding me back from expressing myself? What would happen if I let them go?

_____

_____

_____

_____

_____

_____

_____

_____

_____

_____

_____

_____

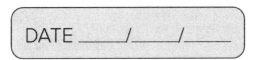

DATE _____/_____/_____

Emotion of the day _____

I'm grateful for _____

131. In what ways can I allow myself to be supported by the people around me? How does the thought of asking for help make me feel?

_____
_____
_____
_____
_____
_____
_____
_____
_____
_____
_____
_____

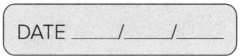

DATE ____ / ____ / ____

Emotion of the day_____

I'm grateful for_____

132. When have I felt invincible in my life? What was that like for me? How long did it last?

_____

_____

_____

_____

_____

_____

_____

_____

_____

_____

_____

_____

_____

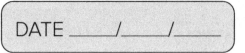

DATE _____/_____/_____

Emotion of the day_____

I'm grateful for_____

133. *Check In! What was journaling this week like for you? Where did you excel and where did you struggle? What new insights came up for you and how are you handling them? Which questions were more challenging than the others? Is there anything else that has happened this week that you'd like to sort through?*

_____

_____

_____

_____

_____

_____

_____

_____

_____

_____

_____

DATE _____/_____/_____

Emotion of the day_____

I'm grateful for_____

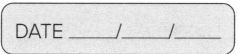

134. When have I listened to my intuition and it worked out in my favor? Was there a time when I ignored it and felt regret? What did I learn from these two situations?

_____

_____

_____

_____

_____

_____

_____

_____

_____

_____

DATE _____ / _____ / _____

Emotion of the day _____

I'm grateful for _____

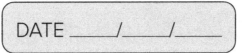

135. When was the last time I celebrated myself? What did I do and what was the reason for celebrating?

_____

_____

_____

_____

_____

_____

_____

_____

_____

_____

_____

_____

_____

DATE _____/_____/_____

Emotion of the day_____

I'm grateful for_____

136. What is my relationship with self-doubt like? How has my self-doubt tried to protect me?

_____

_____

_____

_____

_____

_____

_____

_____

_____

_____

_____

_____

DATE _____/_____/_____

Emotion of the day_____

I'm grateful for_____

137. When have I believed in myself and it worked out? How can I lean on that experience so I can trust in my decisions more often?

_____

_____

_____

_____

_____

_____

_____

_____

_____

_____

_____

_____

Emotion of the day_____

I'm grateful for_____

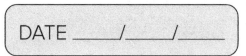

138. Which is worse: Trying and failing or never trying at all? Explain.

_____

_____

_____

_____

_____

_____

_____

_____

_____

_____

_____

_____

DATE _____/_____/_____

Emotion of the day_____

I'm grateful for_____

139. The words I'd like to live my life by are...

_____

_____

_____

_____

_____

_____

_____

_____

_____

_____

_____

_____

_____

DATE _____ / _____ / _____

Emotion of the day _____

I'm grateful for _____

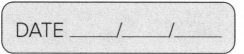

140. *Check In! What was journaling this week like for you? Where did you excel and where did you struggle? What new insights came up for you and how are you handling them? Which questions were more challenging than the others? Is there anything else that has happened this week that you'd like to sort through?*

_____

_____

_____

_____

_____

_____

_____

_____

_____

_____

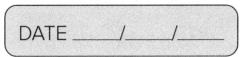

DATE _____ / _____ / _____

Emotion of the day_____

I'm grateful for_____

141. What am I getting out of staying in my current situation?

_____

_____

_____

_____

_____

_____

_____

_____

_____

_____

_____

_____

_____

_____

DATE _____/_____/_____

Emotion of the day_____

I'm grateful for_____

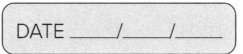

142. Who are the people that improve my life?

_____

_____

_____

_____

_____

_____

_____

_____

_____

_____

_____

_____

_____

DATE _____ / _____ / _____

Emotion of the day_____

I'm grateful for_____

143. Last year, I was so proud of myself when...

_____

_____

_____

_____

_____

_____

_____

_____

_____

_____

_____

_____

_____

DATE _____ / _____ / _____

Emotion of the day _____

I'm grateful for _____

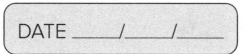

144. What is something special about my little kid self?

_____

_____

_____

_____

_____

_____

_____

_____

_____

_____

_____

_____

_____

_____

DATE _____ / _____ / _____

Emotion of the day _____

I'm grateful for _____

145. What image do I think other people carry about me? Do I agree with them?

_____

_____

_____

_____

_____

_____

_____

_____

_____

_____

_____

_____

_____

_____

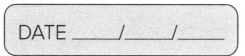

DATE _____/_____/_____

Emotion of the day_____

I'm grateful for_____

146. Is my inner voice truly mine or who's voice is it? Could some-one have influenced it growing up?

_____

_____

_____

_____

_____

_____

_____

_____

_____

_____

_____

_____

DATE _____/_____/_____

Emotion of the day _____

I'm grateful for _____

147. *Check In! What was journaling this week like for you? Where did you excel and where did you struggle? What new insights came up for you and how are you handling them? Which questions were more challenging than the others? Is there anything else that has happened this week that you'd like to sort through?*

_____

_____

_____

_____

_____

_____

_____

_____

_____

_____

DATE _____ / _____ / _____

Emotion of the day _____

I'm grateful for _____

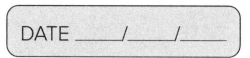

148. When have I opened up to someone and felt accepted? What did I share and who did I share it with?

_____

_____

_____

_____

_____

_____

_____

_____

_____

_____

_____

_____

DATE ____ / ____ / ____

Emotion of the day _____

I'm grateful for _____

149. When was the last time I felt jealous of someone else? What did they have that I wanted? How did I express these feelings?

_____
_____
_____
_____
_____
_____
_____
_____
_____
_____
_____
_____
_____
_____

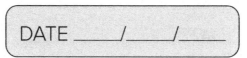

DATE ____/____/____

Emotion of the day_____

I'm grateful for_____

150. How old was I when I first felt angry? What happened?

_____

_____

_____

_____

_____

_____

_____

_____

_____

_____

_____

_____

_____

DATE _____/_____/_____

Emotion of the day _____

I'm grateful for _____

151. When was the last time I felt truly at peace? Where was I and who and what surrounded me for that to be possible?

_____

_____

_____

_____

_____

_____

_____

_____

_____

_____

_____

_____

_____

DATE ____/____/____

Emotion of the day_____

I'm grateful for_____

152. How would I describe my current life to my child self? Which parts would I emphasize and leave out?

_____

_____

_____

_____

_____

_____

_____

_____

_____

_____

_____

_____

_____

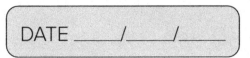

DATE ____ / ____ / ____

Emotion of the day_____

I'm grateful for_____

153. While thinking about a particularly difficult situation I experienced when I was younger, what does it mean for me to have survived this event? What helps me deal with that experience?

_____

_____

_____

_____

_____

_____

_____

_____

_____

_____

_____

_____

Emotion of the day _____

I'm grateful for _____

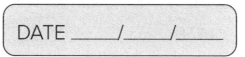

154. *Check In! What was journaling this week like for you? Where did you excel and where did you struggle? What new insights came up for you and how are you handling them? Which questions were more challenging than the others? Is there anything else that has happened this week that you'd like to sort through?*

_____

_____

_____

_____

_____

_____

_____

_____

_____

_____

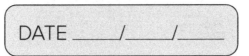

DATE _____/_____/_____

Emotion of the day_____

I'm grateful for_____

155. How has religion impacted my life?

_____

_____

_____

_____

_____

_____

_____

_____

_____

_____

_____

_____

_____

DATE _____ / _____ / _____

Emotion of the day _____

I'm grateful for _____

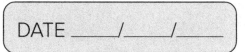

156. How do I feel about spiritual/religious practices? Which ones do I resonate with and which ones am I opposed by?

_____

_____

_____

_____

_____

_____

_____

_____

_____

_____

_____

_____

DATE _____ / _____ / _____

Emotion of the day _____

I'm grateful for _____

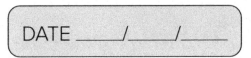

157. Have I ever been harmed by someone who was using religion as a manipulation tool? How do I make sense of that situation?

_____

_____

_____

_____

_____

_____

_____

_____

_____

_____

_____

_____

_____

_____

DATE _____ / _____ / _____

Emotion of the day _____

I'm grateful for _____

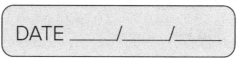

158. Where do I find the most joy in my life? How can I participate in more activities that produce more of that?

_____

_____

_____

_____

_____

_____

_____

_____

_____

_____

_____

_____

DATE _____ / _____ / _____

Emotion of the day_____

I'm grateful for_____

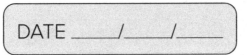

159. What is my purpose in life? How do I know?

_____

_____

_____

_____

_____

_____

_____

_____

_____

_____

_____

_____

_____

DATE ___/___/___

Emotion of the day_____

I'm grateful for_____

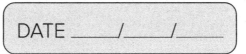

160. What is something I've always wanted in my life but have been too scared to ask for? Where does that fear come from?

_____

_____

_____

_____

_____

_____

_____

_____

_____

_____

_____

_____

_____

DATE _____ / _____ / _____

Emotion of the day_____

I'm grateful for_____

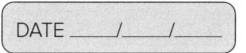

161. *Check In! What was journaling this week like for you? Where did you excel and where did you struggle? What new insights came up for you and how are you handling them? Which questions were more challenging than the others? Is there anything else that has happened this week that you'd like to sort through?*

_____

_____

_____

_____

_____

_____

_____

_____

_____

_____

DATE _____ / _____ / _____

Emotion of the day _____

I'm grateful for _____

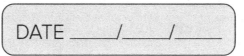

162. When was the last time I felt resentment towards another person? What happened and how was I able to overcome that? If I'm still holding onto it, what's preventing me from letting it go?

_____

_____

_____

_____

_____

_____

_____

_____

_____

_____

_____

DATE _____ / _____ / _____

Emotion of the day _____

I'm grateful for _____

163. Put your hand over your heart and say, "I forgive myself for the challenges I created that harmed other people." What thoughts, feelings, and/or sensations came up when I do that?

_____

_____

_____

_____

_____

_____

_____

_____

_____

_____

_____

_____

DATE ____/____/____

Emotion of the day_____

I'm grateful for_____

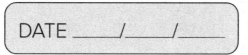

164. Which situations have I felt less than others and what lead to that thought process?

_____

_____

_____

_____

_____

_____

_____

_____

_____

_____

_____

_____

DATE ____ / ____ / ____

Emotion of the day _____

I'm grateful for _____

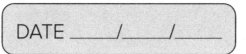

165. Which situations have I felt equal to others and what lead to that thought process?

_____

_____

_____

_____

_____

_____

_____

_____

_____

_____

_____

_____

_____

DATE ____/____/____

Emotion of the day_____

I'm grateful for_____

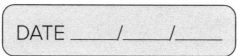

166. Which situations have I felt better than others and what lead to that thought process?

_____

_____

_____

_____

_____

_____

_____

_____

_____

_____

_____

DATE _____/_____/_____

Emotion of the day _____

I'm grateful for _____

167. Which dreams of mine seem possible and others impossible? What makes them attainable or what makes me feel like they may not happen?

_____

_____

_____

_____

_____

_____

_____

_____

_____

_____

_____

DATE _____/_____/_____

Emotion of the day _____

I'm grateful for _____

168. *Check In! What was journaling this week like for you? Where did you excel and where did you struggle? What new insights came up for you and how are you handling them? Which questions were more challenging than the others? Is there anything else that has happened this week that you'd like to sort through?*

_____

_____

_____

_____

_____

_____

_____

_____

_____

_____

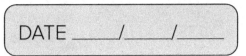

DATE _____/_____/_____

Emotion of the day_____

I'm grateful for_____

169. What were family meals like growing up? How did they affect my relationship with eating as I got older?

_____

_____

_____

_____

_____

_____

_____

_____

_____

_____

_____

_____

_____

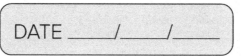

DATE _____/_____/_____

Emotion of the day_____

I'm grateful for_____

170. What is my relationship with food like? Who did I learn my eating habits from and how did that affect the way I look at eating?

_____

_____

_____

_____

_____

_____

_____

_____

_____

_____

_____

_____

DATE ____ / ____ / ____

Emotion of the day_____

I'm grateful for_____

171. Where do I fall victim to other people's opinions? Have I always been this way or is it something I've recently encountered?

_____

_____

_____

_____

_____

_____

_____

_____

_____

_____

_____

_____

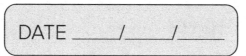

DATE _____/_____/_____

Emotion of the day _____

I'm grateful for _____

172. What body image challenges have I experienced in the past? Where do I still struggle?

_____

_____

_____

_____

_____

_____

_____

_____

_____

_____

_____

_____

DATE ____/____/____

Emotion of the day_____

I'm grateful for_____

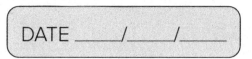

173. In what ways do my limiting beliefs serve me? What do I get out of holding onto them?

_____

_____

_____

_____

_____

_____

_____

_____

_____

_____

_____

_____

DATE _____ / _____ / _____

Emotion of the day _____

I'm grateful for _____

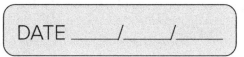

174. When I say out loud, "I love myself", what happens in my body? Do I believe that statement or do I feel resistance to it?

_____

_____

_____

_____

_____

_____

_____

_____

_____

_____

_____

_____

DATE _____ / _____ / _____

Emotion of the day _____

I'm grateful for _____

175. *Check In! What was journaling this week like for you? Where did you excel and where did you struggle? What new insights came up for you and how are you handling them? Which questions were more challenging than the others? Is there anything else that has happened this week that you'd like to sort through?*

_____

_____

_____

_____

_____

_____

_____

_____

_____

_____

DATE _____ / _____ / _____

Emotion of the day _____

I'm grateful for _____

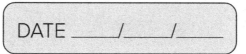

176. How does depression show up in my body? What do I experience?

_____

_____

_____

_____

_____

_____

_____

_____

_____

_____

_____

_____

_____

_____

Emotion of the day_____

I'm grateful for_____

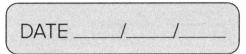

177. Write the words I need to hear the most right now. What is it like looking at this message?

_____

_____

_____

_____

_____

_____

_____

_____

_____

_____

_____

_____

_____

DATE ____/____/____

Emotion of the day _____

I'm grateful for _____

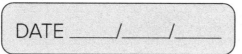

178. What am I currently taking for granted in my life? How can I show more gratitude towards them in the future?

_____
_____
_____
_____
_____
_____
_____
_____
_____
_____
_____
_____
_____

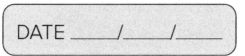

DATE _____ / _____ / _____

Emotion of the day_____

I'm grateful for_____

179. What do I have in my life right now that my past self would be proud to see?

_____

_____

_____

_____

_____

_____

_____

_____

_____

_____

_____

_____

DATE _____ / _____ / _____

Emotion of the day _____

I'm grateful for _____

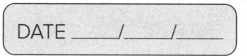

180. How do I respond to criticism? How does that effect my relationships with others around me?

_____

_____

_____

_____

_____

_____

_____

_____

_____

_____

_____

_____

_____

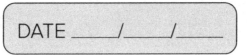

DATE _____ / _____ / _____

Emotion of the day_____

I'm grateful for_____

181. Where do I notice myself shrinking in my life and/or relationships? Who taught me to shrink? Who currently benefits from me shrinking and not speaking up?

_____

_____

_____

_____

_____

_____

_____

_____

_____

_____

_____

_____

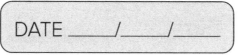

DATE _____/_____/_____

Emotion of the day_____

I'm grateful for_____

182. *Check In! What was journaling this week like for you? Where did you excel and where did you struggle? What new insights came up for you and how are you handling them? Which questions were more challenging than the others? Is there anything else that has happened this week that you'd like to sort through?*

_____

_____

_____

_____

_____

_____

_____

_____

_____

_____

DATE _____ / _____ / _____

Emotion of the day _____

I'm grateful for _____

183. True or False: I need people to accept me to feel comfortable. Why or why not?

_____

_____

_____

_____

_____

_____

_____

_____

_____

_____

_____

_____

_____

DATE _____ / _____ / _____

Emotion of the day _____

I'm grateful for _____

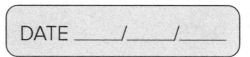

184. How can I tell when I'm making myself a priority? What's that like for me?

_____

_____

_____

_____

_____

_____

_____

_____

_____

_____

_____

_____

DATE _____ / _____ / _____

Emotion of the day_____

I'm grateful for_____

185. I am amazing because...

_____

_____

_____

_____

_____

_____

_____

_____

_____

_____

_____

_____

_____

_____

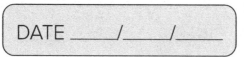

DATE _____/_____/_____

Emotion of the day_____

I'm grateful for_____

186. How does it feel when someone gives me a compliment? How do I normally respond? When was the last time I gave myself a compliment?

_____

_____

_____

_____

_____

_____

_____

_____

_____

_____

_____

_____

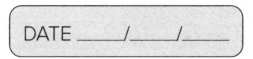

DATE _____ / _____ / _____

Emotion of the day _____

I'm grateful for _____

187. What are some unhealthy coping skills I've adopted that I would like to exchange for healthy ones?

_____

_____

_____

_____

_____

_____

_____

_____

_____

_____

_____

_____

_____

Emotion of the day_____

I'm grateful for_____

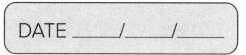

188. How does it feel when someone is upset with me? What happened when I was younger if I made someone angry?

_____

_____

_____

_____

_____

_____

_____

_____

_____

_____

_____

_____

_____

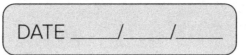

DATE ____/____/____

Emotion of the day _____

I'm grateful for _____

189. *Check In! What was journaling this week like for you? Where did you excel and where did you struggle? What new insights came up for you and how are you handling them? Which questions were more challenging than the others? Is there anything else that has happened this week that you'd like to sort through?*

_____

_____

_____

_____

_____

_____

_____

_____

_____

_____

DATE _____ / _____ / _____

Emotion of the day _____

I'm grateful for _____

190. Set a timer for at least 3 minutes and sit your pretty face in front of a mirror and just look at yourself. Do your best not to critique or judge, just be present. What comes up for you? Do any emotions surface? What's your experience with this exercise like?

_____

_____

_____

_____

_____

_____

_____

_____

_____

_____

_____

DATE ____ / ____ / ____

Emotion of the day _____

I'm grateful for _____

191. What are some negative and hurtful things I have told myself when I've made a mistake? Now imagine a picture of me as a young child and tell those same negative judgements to that younger version, what does that feel like? Has anything changed?

_____

_____

_____

_____

_____

_____

_____

_____

_____

_____

_____

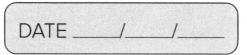

DATE _____/_____/_____

Emotion of the day _____

I'm grateful for _____

192. Where do I notice expansion in my life and/or relationships? What do I feel is allowing me to expand and where did I learn how to do that?

_____

_____

_____

_____

_____

_____

_____

_____

_____

_____

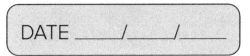

DATE _____ / _____ / _____

Emotion of the day_____

I'm grateful for_____

193. In what areas of my life do I find myself making excuses for why I either am or am not doing things more effectively? Have I always done this or is this new? How are these excuses serving me?

_____

_____

_____

_____

_____

_____

_____

_____

_____

_____

_____

DATE _____/_____/_____

Emotion of the day_____

I'm grateful for_____

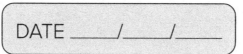

194. How would my life look without the anger/anxiety/depression I'm holding on to?

_____

_____

_____

_____

_____

_____

_____

_____

_____

_____

_____

_____

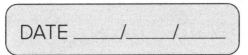

DATE _____ / _____ / _____

Emotion of the day_____

I'm grateful for_____

195. Who am I?

_____

_____

_____

_____

_____

_____

_____

_____

_____

_____

_____

_____

_____

_____

_____

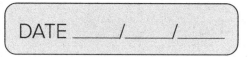

DATE _____/_____/_____

Emotion of the day_____

I'm grateful for_____

196. *Check In! What was journaling this week like for you? Where did you excel and where did you struggle? What new insights came up for you and how are you handling them? Which questions were more challenging than the others? Is there anything else that has happened this week that you'd like to sort through?*

_____

_____

_____

_____

_____

_____

_____

_____

_____

_____

DATE _____/_____/_____

Emotion of the day_____

I'm grateful for_____

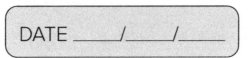

197. What trauma responses have I created to help myself survive? Are they still needed?

_____

_____

_____

_____

_____

_____

_____

_____

_____

_____

_____

_____

_____

DATE _____/_____/_____

Emotion of the day_____

I'm grateful for_____

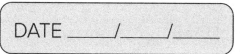

198. What is one trait I see in other people that I can't stand? When in my life have I displayed this characteristic?

_____

_____

_____

_____

_____

_____

_____

_____

_____

_____

_____

DATE _____ / _____ / _____

Emotion of the day _____

I'm grateful for _____

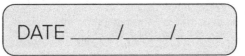

199. Explore this statement: I am easily influenced or swayed by the opinions and beliefs of others. I find it hard to assert my own voice and figure out what is theirs vs mine.

_____

_____

_____

_____

_____

_____

_____

_____

_____

_____

_____

DATE _____/_____/_____

Emotion of the day_____

I'm grateful for_____

200. Agree or Disagree? I regularly downplay how I feel or what I'm really thinking for the sake of others. Explain.

_____

_____

_____

_____

_____

_____

_____

_____

_____

_____

_____

_____

_____

DATE _____/_____/_____

Emotion of the day_____

I'm grateful for_____

201. What is my definition of failure? Who taught me that belief system?

_____

_____

_____

_____

_____

_____

_____

_____

_____

_____

_____

_____

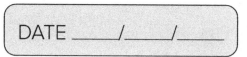

DATE _____/_____/_____

Emotion of the day_____

I'm grateful for_____

202. If there were no negative consequences, what would I do today? How long have I been wanting to do that?

_____
_____
_____
_____
_____
_____
_____
_____
_____
_____
_____
_____

DATE _____ / _____ / _____

Emotion of the day _____

I'm grateful for _____

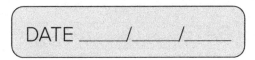

203. *Check In! What was journaling this week like for you? Where did you excel and where did you struggle? What new insights came up for you and how are you handling them? Which questions were more challenging than the others? Is there anything else that has happened this week that you'd like to sort through?*

_____

_____

_____

_____

_____

_____

_____

_____

_____

_____

DATE _____/_____/_____

Emotion of the day _____

I'm grateful for _____

204. Do I feel I'm only as good as my last achievement? Why or why not? How did my parents treat me when I didn't meet one of their expectations?

_____

_____

_____

_____

_____

_____

_____

_____

_____

_____

_____

DATE ____/____/____

Emotion of the day_____

I'm grateful for_____

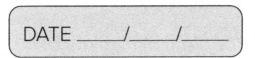

205. In what ways do I self-sabotage? How often am I doing this consciously versus subconsciously?

_____

_____

_____

_____

_____

_____

_____

_____

_____

_____

_____

_____

_____

DATE _____ / _____ / _____

Emotion of the day _____

I'm grateful for _____

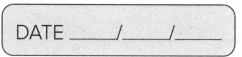

206. What do I wish I could let go of? What would my life look like if I did?

_____

_____

_____

_____

_____

_____

_____

_____

_____

_____

_____

_____

_____

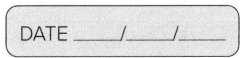

DATE _____ / _____ / _____

Emotion of the day_____

I'm grateful for_____

207. Where in my life can I stop playing the victim and take responsibility for my part of the mess?

_____

_____

_____

_____

_____

_____

_____

_____

_____

_____

_____

_____

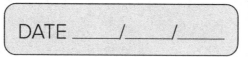

DATE _____/_____/_____

Emotion of the day _____

I'm grateful for _____

208. What is the biggest lie I consistently tell myself and why? How does that serve me?

_____
_____
_____
_____
_____
_____
_____
_____
_____
_____
_____
_____

DATE ____ / ____ / ____

Emotion of the day_____

I'm grateful for_____

209. What does integrity mean to me and where in my life have I struggled maintaining it?

_____

_____

_____

_____

_____

_____

_____

_____

_____

_____

_____

_____

_____

DATE ____/____/____

Emotion of the day_____

I'm grateful for_____

210. *Check In! What was journaling this week like for you? Where did you excel and where did you struggle? What new insights came up for you and how are you handling them? Which questions were more challenging than the others? Is there anything else that has happened this week that you'd like to sort through?*

_____

_____

_____

_____

_____

_____

_____

_____

_____

_____

DATE ____ / ____ / ____

Emotion of the day _____

I'm grateful for _____

211. What does femininity mean to me?

_____
_____
_____
_____
_____
_____
_____
_____
_____
_____
_____
_____
_____
_____

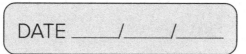

DATE _____/_____/_____

Emotion of the day _____

I'm grateful for _____

212. What does masculinity mean to me?

_____

_____

_____

_____

_____

_____

_____

_____

_____

_____

_____

_____

_____

_____

_____

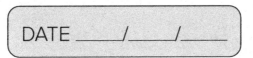

DATE _____/_____/_____

Emotion of the day_____

I'm grateful for_____

213. What actions can someone take to make me feel seen?

_____

_____

_____

_____

_____

_____

_____

_____

_____

_____

_____

_____

_____

_____

DATE ____ / ____ / ____

Emotion of the day_____

I'm grateful for_____

214. How do I like people to communicate hard things to me?

_____

_____

_____

_____

_____

_____

_____

_____

_____

_____

_____

_____

_____

DATE _____ / _____ / _____

Emotion of the day _____

I'm grateful for _____

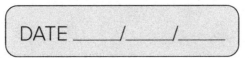

215. What's preventing me from being successful in
my relationships?

_____

_____

_____

_____

_____

_____

_____

_____

_____

_____

_____

_____

_____

DATE ____/____/____

Emotion of the day _____

I'm grateful for _____

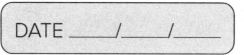

216. How would someone who loves themselves communicate towards themselves?

_____

_____

_____

_____

_____

_____

_____

_____

_____

_____

_____

DATE _____/_____/_____

Emotion of the day_____

I'm grateful for_____

217. *Check In! What was journaling this week like for you? Where did you excel and where did you struggle? What new insights came up for you and how are you handling them? Which questions were more challenging than the others? Is there anything else that has happened this week that you'd like to sort through?*

_____

_____

_____

_____

_____

_____

_____

_____

_____

_____

DATE _____ / _____ / _____

Emotion of the day _____

I'm grateful for _____

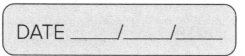

218. What frightens me about relationships? When did I learn and who taught me to be afraid of these things?

_____

_____

_____

_____

_____

_____

_____

_____

_____

_____

_____

_____

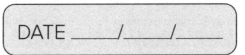

DATE ____/____/____

Emotion of the day _____

I'm grateful for _____

219. How do I like to discuss difficult topics? What helps me become a more effective communicator?

_____
_____
_____
_____
_____
_____
_____
_____
_____
_____
_____
_____
_____

DATE _____/_____/_____

Emotion of the day _____

I'm grateful for _____

220. What does intimacy look like, feel like, and sound like to me?

_____

_____

_____

_____

_____

_____

_____

_____

_____

_____

_____

_____

_____

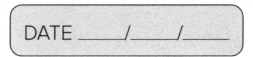

DATE _____ / _____ / _____

Emotion of the day_____

I'm grateful for_____

221. If I could gain clarity about (situation), then I would...

_____

_____

_____

_____

_____

_____

_____

_____

_____

_____

_____

_____

_____

_____

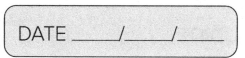

DATE _____/_____/_____

Emotion of the day_____

I'm grateful for_____

222. Where am I trying to fix situations that aren't my responsibility to fix?

_____

_____

_____

_____

_____

_____

_____

_____

_____

_____

_____

_____

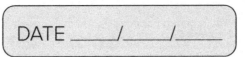

DATE ____/____/____

Emotion of the day_____

I'm grateful for_____

223. Finish these sentences. "I am..." "People are..." "The world is..."

_____

_____

_____

_____

_____

_____

_____

_____

_____

_____

_____

_____

_____

_____

DATE ____ / ____ / ____

Emotion of the day_____

I'm grateful for_____

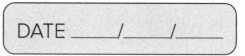

224. Check In! What was journaling this week like for you? Where did you excel and where did you struggle? What new insights came up for you and how are you handling them? Which questions were more challenging than the others? Is there anything else that has happened this week that you'd like to sort through?

_____

_____

_____

_____

_____

_____

_____

_____

_____

_____

DATE ____/____/____

Emotion of the day_____

I'm grateful for_____

225. What's the ugliest part of myself and how do I know it's ugly? What would happen if someone caught a glimpse of it? Who told me it was ugly?

_____

_____

_____

_____

_____

_____

_____

_____

_____

_____

_____

_____

DATE _____/_____/_____

Emotion of the day_____

I'm grateful for_____

226. What behaviors in other people upset me the most and why? Have I ever participated in them and if so, why did I make those choices?

_____

_____

_____

_____

_____

_____

_____

_____

_____

_____

_____

_____

DATE _____/_____/_____

Emotion of the day _____

I'm grateful for _____

227. Do I like to deal with my problems right away, like to wait until I've processed them first, or pretend like they don't exist and hope they go away on their own? How does this method serve me?

_____

_____

_____

_____

_____

_____

_____

_____

_____

_____

_____

_____

DATE _____ / _____ / _____

Emotion of the day _____

I'm grateful for _____

228. In what ways can I add more joy into my life?

_____

_____

_____

_____

_____

_____

_____

_____

_____

_____

_____

_____

_____

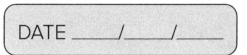

DATE _____/_____/_____

Emotion of the day_____

I'm grateful for_____

229. What opportunities do I need to take advantage of now to become a healthier version of myself?

_____

_____

_____

_____

_____

_____

_____

_____

_____

_____

_____

_____

DATE _____/_____/_____

Emotion of the day _____

I'm grateful for _____

230. If I could let go of the thought _____, I could accomplish _____. Explain.

_____

_____

_____

_____

_____

_____

_____

_____

_____

_____

_____

_____

_____

_____

DATE _____ / _____ / _____

Emotion of the day _____

I'm grateful for _____

231. *Check In! What was journaling this week like for you? Where did you excel and where did you struggle? What new insights came up for you and how are you handling them? Which questions were more challenging than the others? Is there anything else that has happened this week that you'd like to sort through?*

_____

_____

_____

_____

_____

_____

_____

_____

_____

_____

DATE ____ / ____ / ____

Emotion of the day _____

I'm grateful for _____

232. What does "living my best life" look, sound, and feel like to me?

_____
_____
_____
_____
_____
_____
_____
_____
_____
_____
_____
_____
_____
_____

DATE _____/_____/_____

Emotion of the day_____

I'm grateful for_____

233. How can I regain hope that life will get easier in the future?

_____

_____

_____

_____

_____

_____

_____

_____

_____

_____

_____

_____

_____

_____

Emotion of the day_____

I'm grateful for_____

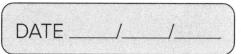

234. How come I haven't given up by now? What keeps me moving forward?

_____

_____

_____

_____

_____

_____

_____

_____

_____

_____

_____

_____

DATE _____/_____/_____

Emotion of the day_____

I'm grateful for_____

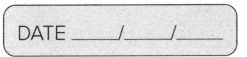

235. What do I want to be when I grow up? Is that different than what my 10 year old self would have said?

_____

_____

_____

_____

_____

_____

_____

_____

_____

_____

_____

_____

DATE _____/_____/_____

Emotion of the day_____

I'm grateful for_____

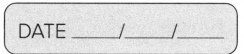

236. Looking back, what has it taken to make the positive changes I have already made in my life?

_____

_____

_____

_____

_____

_____

_____

_____

_____

_____

_____

_____

DATE _____ / _____ / _____

Emotion of the day_____

I'm grateful for_____

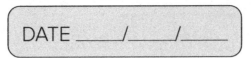

237. Who do I think looks up to me? When I make my decisions, how do they impact that person?

_____

_____

_____

_____

_____

_____

_____

_____

_____

_____

_____

_____

_____

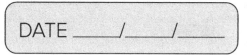

DATE _____/_____/_____

Emotion of the day _____

I'm grateful for _____

238. *Check In! What was journaling this week like for you? Where did you excel and where did you struggle? What new insights came up for you and how are you handling them? Which questions were more challenging than the others? Is there anything else that has happened this week that you'd like to sort through?*

_____

_____

_____

_____

_____

_____

_____

_____

DATE _____ / _____ / _____

Emotion of the day _____

I'm grateful for _____

239. What trauma responses have I created to help me survive?
How are they still necessary?

_____

_____

_____

_____

_____

_____

_____

_____

_____

_____

_____

_____

_____

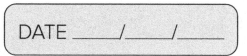

DATE ____/____/____

Emotion of the day_____

I'm grateful for_____

240. What makes me feel jealous? Where am I lacking what others have and why do I feel like I need it to be happy?

_____

_____

_____

_____

_____

_____

_____

_____

_____

_____

_____

_____

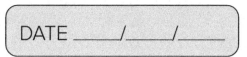

DATE _____/_____/_____

Emotion of the day_____

I'm grateful for_____

241. What are some things that are easy for me to do that others might find difficult? How do I honor those skills in my life?

_____

_____

_____

_____

_____

_____

_____

_____

_____

_____

_____

Emotion of the day_____

I'm grateful for_____

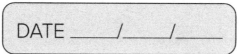

242. How do I define my personal and professional success? How are they different and the same?

_____

_____

_____

_____

_____

_____

_____

_____

_____

_____

_____

DATE _____ / _____ / _____

Emotion of the day _____

I'm grateful for _____

243. What areas in my life do I find myself getting more defensive than others? How did I learn to protect this space?

_____

_____

_____

_____

_____

_____

_____

_____

_____

_____

_____

_____

_____

DATE _____ / _____ / _____

Emotion of the day_____

I'm grateful for_____

244. How often do I doubt myself? How has this served me in my life?

_____

_____

_____

_____

_____

_____

_____

_____

_____

_____

_____

_____

_____

_____

DATE _____/_____/_____

Emotion of the day_____

I'm grateful for_____

245. *Check In! What was journaling this week like for you? Where did you excel and where did you struggle? What new insights came up for you and how are you handling them? Which questions were more challenging than the others? Is there anything else that has happened this week that you'd like to sort through?*

_____

_____

_____

_____

_____

_____

_____

_____

_____

_____

_____

DATE _____ / _____ / _____

Emotion of the day _____

I'm grateful for _____

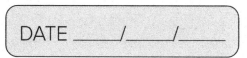

246. If my body could talk, it would say...

_____

_____

_____

_____

_____

_____

_____

_____

_____

_____

_____

_____

_____

_____

DATE _____/_____/_____

Emotion of the day_____

I'm grateful for_____

247. How does anxiety show up in my body? Has it always been this way? What's changed?

_____

_____

_____

_____

_____

_____

_____

_____

_____

_____

_____

_____

_____

_____

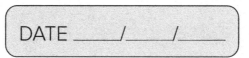

DATE _____/_____/_____

Emotion of the day_____

I'm grateful for_____

248. What kinds of thoughts do I have while I'm trying to go to sleep at night? How are they affecting my sleep?

_____

_____

_____

_____

_____

_____

_____

_____

_____

_____

_____

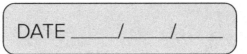

DATE ____ / ____ / ____

Emotion of the day_____

I'm grateful for_____

249. What do I wish I would have seen or felt more of growing up?

_____

_____

_____

_____

_____

_____

_____

_____

_____

_____

_____

_____

_____

_____

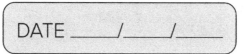

DATE _____/_____/_____

Emotion of the day_____

I'm grateful for_____

250. How do I feel about asking for help? In what areas am I better at asking versus others?

_____

_____

_____

_____

_____

_____

_____

_____

_____

_____

_____

_____

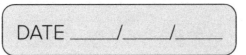

DATE _____ / _____ / _____

Emotion of the day_____

I'm grateful for_____

251. What are some limiting beliefs I would like to let go of?

_____

_____

_____

_____

_____

_____

_____

_____

_____

_____

_____

_____

_____

DATE ____/____/____

Emotion of the day_____

I'm grateful for_____

252. *Check In! What was journaling this week like for you? Where did you excel and where did you struggle? What new insights came up for you and how are you handling them? Which questions were more challenging than the others? Is there anything else that has happened this week that you'd like to sort through?*

_____

_____

_____

_____

_____

_____

_____

_____

_____

_____

_____

Emotion of the day_____

I'm grateful for_____

253. I'm feeling stuck right now because...

_____

_____

_____

_____

_____

_____

_____

_____

_____

_____

_____

_____

_____

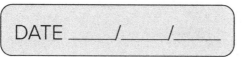

DATE ____/____/____

Emotion of the day_____

I'm grateful for_____

254. In what areas in my life do I struggle with being kind to myself? Where did I learn this pattern?

_____

_____

_____

_____

_____

_____

_____

_____

_____

_____

_____

_____

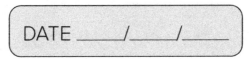

DATE _____ / _____ / _____

Emotion of the day _____

I'm grateful for _____

255. Where do I struggle with allowing people to support me? How can I make moves to work on that?

_____

_____

_____

_____

_____

_____

_____

_____

_____

_____

_____

_____

_____

DATE _____/_____/_____

Emotion of the day _____

I'm grateful for _____

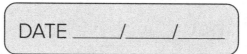

256. What's my biggest struggle when it comes to being consistent and sticking to my goals? How can I make moves to work on them?

_____

_____

_____

_____

_____

_____

_____

_____

_____

_____

_____

DATE ____/____/____

Emotion of the day_____

I'm grateful for_____

257. What is the loudest insecurity I have right now and who instilled it in me?

_____

_____

_____

_____

_____

_____

_____

_____

_____

_____

_____

_____

_____

DATE _____/_____/_____

Emotion of the day_____

I'm grateful for_____

258. When I hear, "Love yourself first", what is my initial reaction and where do I feel it in my body?

_____   _____

_____

_____

_____

_____

_____

_____

_____

_____

_____

_____

_____

_____

DATE _____/_____/_____

Emotion of the day _____

I'm grateful for _____

259. *Check In! What was journaling this week like for you? Where did you excel and where did you struggle? What new insights came up for you and how are you handling them? Which questions were more challenging than the others? Is there anything else that has happened this week that you'd like to sort through?*

_____

_____

_____

_____

_____

_____

_____

_____

_____

_____

DATE _____/_____/_____

Emotion of the day_____

I'm grateful for_____

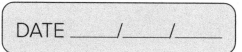

260. What does "being a man" mean to me?

_____

_____

_____

_____

_____

_____

_____

_____

_____

_____

_____

_____

_____

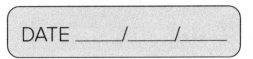

DATE _____ / _____ / _____

Emotion of the day_____

I'm grateful for_____

261. What does "being a woman" mean to me?

_____
_____
_____
_____
_____
_____
_____
_____
_____
_____
_____
_____
_____
_____
_____

Emotion of the day _____

I'm grateful for _____

262. What does "being a child" mean to me?

_____

_____

_____

_____

_____

_____

_____

_____

_____

_____

_____

_____

_____

DATE _____/_____/_____

Emotion of the day _____

I'm grateful for _____

263. What does "being a bad person" mean to me?

_____

_____

_____

_____

_____

_____

_____

_____

_____

_____

_____

_____

_____

DATE _____/_____/_____

Emotion of the day _____

I'm grateful for _____

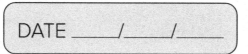

264. What does "being a good person" mean to me?

_____

_____

_____

_____

_____

_____

_____

_____

_____

_____

_____

_____

_____

DATE _____ / _____ / _____

Emotion of the day _____

I'm grateful for _____

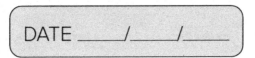

265. What does "being a healthy person" mean to me?

_____

_____

_____

_____

_____

_____

_____

_____

_____

_____

_____

_____

_____

_____

DATE _____ / _____ / _____

Emotion of the day _____

I'm grateful for _____

266. *Check In! What was journaling this week like for you? Where did you excel and where did you struggle? What new insights came up for you and how are you handling them? Which questions were more challenging than the others? Is there anything else that has happened this week that you'd like to sort through?*

_____

_____

_____

_____

_____

_____

_____

_____

_____

_____

_____

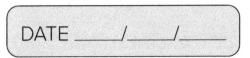

DATE ____ / ____ / ____

Emotion of the day_____

I'm grateful for_____

267. What is my relationship with money like right now compared to what it's been in the past? In what areas do I struggle and succeed?

_____
_____
_____
_____
_____
_____
_____
_____
_____
_____
_____
_____
_____
_____

DATE ____/____/____

Emotion of the day _____

I'm grateful for _____

268. What could I achieve without the barriers I have put in my life? Do these barriers stem from society, family, and/or self-inflicted?

_____

_____

_____

_____

_____

_____

_____

_____

_____

_____

_____

_____

DATE _____/_____/_____

Emotion of the day_____

I'm grateful for_____

269. How often do I doubt the capabilities of others and how has this served me in the past?

_____

_____

_____

_____

_____

_____

_____

_____

_____

_____

_____

_____

_____

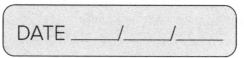

DATE _____/_____/_____

Emotion of the day_____

I'm grateful for_____

270. Pick 10 words to describe myself with. What is it like looking at these words and how many are negative and positive?

_____

_____

_____

_____

_____

_____

_____

_____

_____

_____

_____

_____

DATE _____ / _____ / _____

Emotion of the day _____

I'm grateful for _____

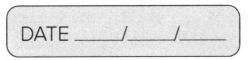

271. Why do I matter? If I answered, "I don't", who taught me that and how is that thought serving me? If I explained why I matter, who helped instill those thoughts in me?

_____

_____

_____

_____

_____

_____

_____

_____

_____

_____

_____

_____

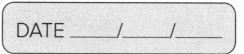

DATE ____/____/____

Emotion of the day_____

I'm grateful for_____

272. What does unconditional love look like for me? Have there been relationships where I still feel that love towards them but had to decide I couldn't be with them?

_____

_____

_____

_____

_____

_____

_____

_____

_____

_____

DATE ____ / ____ / ____

Emotion of the day _____

I'm grateful for _____

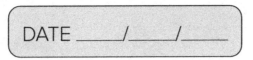

273. *Check In! What was journaling this week like for you? Where did you excel and where did you struggle? What new insights came up for you and how are you handling them? Which questions were more challenging than the others? Is there anything else that has happened this week that you'd like to sort through?*

_____

_____

_____

_____

_____

_____

_____

_____

_____

_____

_____

DATE ____/____/____

Emotion of the day _____

I'm grateful for _____

274. What is the difference between my favorite version of myself and my best self?

_____

_____

_____

_____

_____

_____

_____

_____

_____

_____

_____

DATE _____ / _____ / _____

Emotion of the day _____

I'm grateful for _____

275. Where in my life do I struggle with establishing and maintaining boundaries? Why is that?

_____

_____

_____

_____

_____

_____

_____

_____

_____

_____

_____

_____

DATE ____ / ____ / ____

Emotion of the day _____

I'm grateful for _____

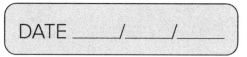

276. When do I feel the most alive? Describe the emotions and what happens in my body.

_____

_____

_____

_____

_____

_____

_____

_____

_____

_____

_____

_____

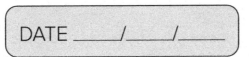

DATE _____/_____/_____

Emotion of the day _____

I'm grateful for _____

277. What is the meaning of living each day?

_____
_____
_____
_____
_____
_____
_____
_____
_____
_____
_____
_____
_____
_____

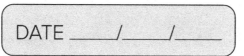

DATE _____ / _____ / _____

Emotion of the day _____

I'm grateful for _____

278. What makes me feel special and important?

_____

_____

_____

_____

_____

_____

_____

_____

_____

_____

_____

_____

_____

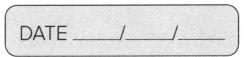

DATE _____ / _____ / _____

Emotion of the day_____

I'm grateful for_____

279. How has music been a part of my healing journey? Do I have certain go to artists for different feelings or experiences?

_____

_____

_____

_____

_____

_____

_____

_____

_____

_____

_____

_____

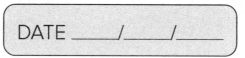

DATE _____/_____/_____

Emotion of the day_____

I'm grateful for_____

280. *Check In! What was journaling this week like for you? Where did you excel and where did you struggle? What new insights came up for you and how are you handling them? Which questions were more challenging than the others? Is there anything else that has happened this week that you'd like to sort through?*

_____

_____

_____

_____

_____

_____

_____

_____

_____

_____

_____

DATE _____/_____/_____

Emotion of the day_____

I'm grateful for_____

281. When I die, how would I like to be remembered?

_____

_____

_____

_____

_____

_____

_____

_____

_____

_____

_____

_____

_____

_____

DATE ____ / ____ / ____

Emotion of the day _____

I'm grateful for _____

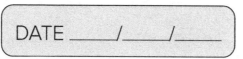

282. What is my relationship with grief like? How has grief impacted me throughout my life?

_____

_____

_____

_____

_____

_____

_____

_____

_____

_____

_____

_____

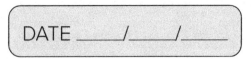

DATE ____ / ____ / ____

Emotion of the day _____

I'm grateful for _____

283. What life lessons do I feel I've learned "too late" in life? What would have changed if I had learned them sooner?

_____

_____

_____

_____

_____

_____

_____

_____

_____

_____

_____

_____

DATE _____/_____/_____

Emotion of the day_____

I'm grateful for_____

284. What scares me the most in this life? Where did I learn to be afraid of that?

_____

_____

_____

_____

_____

_____

_____

_____

_____

_____

_____

_____

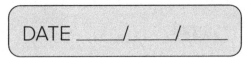

DATE ____/____/____

Emotion of the day _____

I'm grateful for _____

285. How will I know that I am doing justice to myself and my possibilities despite what was done to me?

_____

_____

_____

_____

_____

_____

_____

_____

_____

_____

_____

_____

DATE _____/_____/_____

Emotion of the day_____

I'm grateful for_____

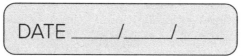

286. What would my best friends say my strengths are? Do I agree with them?

_____

_____

_____

_____

_____

_____

_____

_____

_____

_____

_____

_____

DATE _____/_____/_____

Emotion of the day_____

I'm grateful for_____

287. *Check In! What was journaling this week like for you? Where did you excel and where did you struggle? What new insights came up for you and how are you handling them? Which questions were more challenging than the others? Is there anything else that has happened this week that you'd like to sort through?*

_____

_____

_____

_____

_____

_____

_____

_____

_____

_____

DATE _____/_____/_____

Emotion of the day _____

I'm grateful for _____

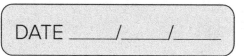

288. How have animals impacted my life? How do they continue to do so?

_____

_____

_____

_____

_____

_____

_____

_____

_____

_____

_____

_____

DATE ___/___/___

Emotion of the day _____

I'm grateful for _____

289. I wouldn't be alive today if it weren't for...

_____

_____

_____

_____

_____

_____

_____

_____

_____

_____

_____

_____

_____

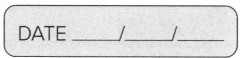

DATE _____/_____/_____

Emotion of the day_____

I'm grateful for_____

290. What kind words do I provide to my friends that I could give to myself more often?

_____

_____

_____

_____

_____

_____

_____

_____

_____

_____

_____

_____

DATE _____/_____/_____

Emotion of the day_____

I'm grateful for_____

291. In what ways have I participated in self-harm either emotionally or physically? Could being in toxic relationships be a version of self-harm?

_____

_____

_____

_____

_____

_____

_____

_____

_____

_____

DATE ____/____/____

Emotion of the day_____

I'm grateful for_____

292. What year in school was the most difficult to live through? What made it challenging and how did I persevere?

_____

_____

_____

_____

_____

_____

_____

_____

_____

_____

_____

_____

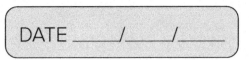

DATE _____ / _____ / _____

Emotion of the day _____

I'm grateful for _____

293. When have I put the needs of others before my own? How did that benefit the relationship? How did that hinder the relationship I have with myself?

_____

_____

_____

_____

_____

_____

_____

_____

_____

_____

_____

_____

DATE _____ / _____ / _____

Emotion of the day _____

I'm grateful for _____

294. *Check In! What was journaling this week like for you? Where did you excel and where did you struggle? What new insights came up for you and how are you handling them? Which questions were more challenging than the others? Is there anything else that has happened this week that you'd like to sort through?*

_____

_____

_____

_____

_____

_____

_____

_____

_____

_____

_____

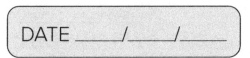

DATE ____/____/____

Emotion of the day_____

I'm grateful for_____

295. Name 3 habits I'd like to break in the next year and how can I start working towards letting them go?

_____

_____

_____

_____

_____

_____

_____

_____

_____

_____

_____

_____

_____

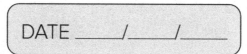

DATE _____/_____/_____

Emotion of the day_____

I'm grateful for_____

296. I feel energized after spending time with... I feel energized doing...

_____
_____
_____
_____
_____
_____
_____
_____
_____
_____
_____
_____

DATE ____/____/____

Emotion of the day_____

I'm grateful for_____

297. I know that I am loved because...

_____

_____

_____

_____

_____

_____

_____

_____

_____

_____

_____

_____

_____

_____

DATE _____ / _____ / _____

Emotion of the day_____

I'm grateful for_____

298. It makes me happy when people say that I...

_____

_____

_____

_____

_____

_____

_____

_____

_____

_____

_____

_____

_____

_____

DATE _____ / _____ / _____

Emotion of the day _____

I'm grateful for _____

299. I feel drained after spending time with... I feel drained after doing...

_____

_____

_____

_____

_____

_____

_____

_____

_____

_____

_____

_____

_____

DATE _____ / _____ / _____

Emotion of the day _____

I'm grateful for _____

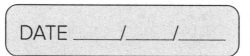

300. I feel content when I...

_____
_____
_____
_____
_____
_____
_____
_____
_____
_____
_____
_____
_____
_____

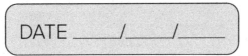

DATE _____/_____/_____

Emotion of the day_____

I'm grateful for_____

301. *Check In! What was journaling this week like for you? Where did you excel and where did you struggle? What new insights came up for you and how are you handling them? Which questions were more challenging than the others? Is there anything else that has happened this week that you'd like to sort through?*

_____

_____

_____

_____

_____

_____

_____

_____

_____

_____

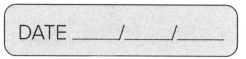

DATE ____/____/____

Emotion of the day_____

I'm grateful for_____

302. Do I ever find myself trying to manipulate others in an attempt to protect myself or to get my needs met? When/where have I learned this technique?

_____
_____
_____
_____
_____
_____
_____
_____
_____
_____
_____
_____

DATE _____ / _____ / _____

Emotion of the day _____

I'm grateful for _____

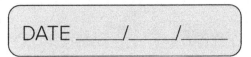

303. If I respected myself, I would...

_____

_____

_____

_____

_____

_____

_____

_____

_____

_____

_____

_____

_____

_____

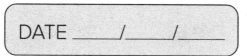

DATE _____ / _____ / _____

Emotion of the day _____

I'm grateful for _____

304. How am I a good person? In what ways do I care for my loved ones?

_____

_____

_____

_____

_____

_____

_____

_____

_____

_____

_____

DATE ____ / ____ / ____

Emotion of the day _____

I'm grateful for _____

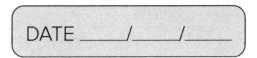

305. What is the best thing about being _____ years old?

_____

_____

_____

_____

_____

_____

_____

_____

_____

_____

_____

_____

_____

_____

DATE ____/____/____

Emotion of the day _____

I'm grateful for _____

306. In what ways am I jealous of the kids growing up in this world?

_____

_____

_____

_____

_____

_____

_____

_____

_____

_____

_____

_____

_____

DATE _____/_____/_____

Emotion of the day_____

I'm grateful for_____

307. In what ways am I saddened for the kids growing up in this world?

_____

_____

_____

_____

_____

_____

_____

_____

_____

_____

_____

_____

_____

DATE _____/_____/_____

Emotion of the day _____

I'm grateful for _____

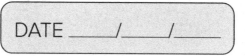

308. *Check In! What was journaling this week like for you? Where did you excel and where did you struggle? What new insights came up for you and how are you handling them? Which questions were more challenging than the others? Is there anything else that has happened this week that you'd like to sort through?*

_____

_____

_____

_____

_____

_____

_____

_____

_____

_____

DATE _____/_____/_____

Emotion of the day_____

I'm grateful for_____

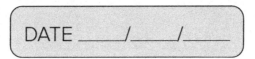

309. What do people often compliment me for? How does it make me feel when I hear them?

_____

_____

_____

_____

_____

_____

_____

_____

_____

_____

_____

_____

_____

DATE ____ / ____ / ____

Emotion of the day _____

I'm grateful for _____

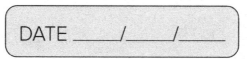

310. What does self-compassion mean to me? How can I provide myself more of that on a regular basis?

_____

_____

_____

_____

_____

_____

_____

_____

_____

_____

_____

_____

_____

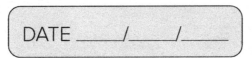

DATE _____ / _____ / _____

Emotion of the day_____

I'm grateful for_____

311. How come I haven't given up by now? What keeps me moving forward?

_____

_____

_____

_____

_____

_____

_____

_____

_____

_____

_____

_____

_____

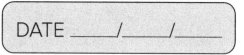

DATE _____/_____/_____

Emotion of the day_____

I'm grateful for_____

312. What will be the signs of progress in my life? What will it feel like when I notice these signs?

_____

_____

_____

_____

_____

_____

_____

_____

_____

_____

_____

_____

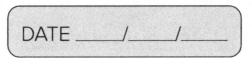

DATE _____ / _____ / _____

Emotion of the day_____

I'm grateful for_____

313. Who will be the first person to notice the positive changes I've made in my life? How will I know they've noticed?

_____

_____

_____

_____

_____

_____

_____

_____

_____

_____

_____

_____

_____

DATE _____/_____/_____

Emotion of the day_____

I'm grateful for_____

314. What would be the best question I could be asked right now? How would this question help me and make me feel?

_____

_____

_____

_____

_____

_____

_____

_____

_____

_____

_____

_____

DATE _____ / _____ / _____

Emotion of the day _____

I'm grateful for _____

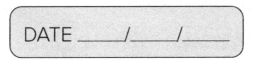

315. *Check In! What was journaling this week like for you? Where did you excel and where did you struggle? What new insights came up for you and how are you handling them? Which questions were more challenging than the others? Is there anything else that has happened this week that you'd like to sort through?*

_____

_____

_____

_____

_____

_____

_____

_____

_____

_____

_____

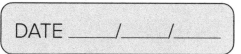

DATE _____/_____/_____

Emotion of the day _____

I'm grateful for _____

316. When I'm stressed, how can I comfort myself? How sustainable are these ways of comforting?

_____
_____
_____
_____
_____
_____
_____
_____
_____
_____
_____
_____

DATE _____/_____/_____

Emotion of the day_____

I'm grateful for_____

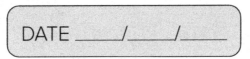

317. What would a healthier version of myself look like, sound like, and feel like?

_____

_____

_____

_____

_____

_____

_____

_____

_____

_____

_____

_____

_____

DATE _____/_____/_____

Emotion of the day_____

I'm grateful for_____

318. What new hobbies or activities does my ideal future self have?

_____

_____

_____

_____

_____

_____

_____

_____

_____

_____

_____

_____

_____

DATE _____ / _____ / _____

Emotion of the day _____

I'm grateful for _____

319. What would a life of self-acceptance feel and look like for me?

_____
_____
_____
_____
_____
_____
_____
_____
_____
_____
_____
_____
_____
_____

DATE _____ / _____ / _____

Emotion of the day_____

I'm grateful for_____

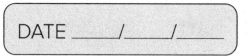

320. What is something I can do today that my future self would be proud of? Why would that make them proud?

_____

_____

_____

_____

_____

_____

_____

_____

_____

_____

_____

DATE _____ / _____ / _____

Emotion of the day _____

I'm grateful for _____

321. One of my biggest goals is...

_____

_____

_____

_____

_____

_____

_____

_____

_____

_____

_____

_____

_____

DATE _____/_____/_____

Emotion of the day_____

I'm grateful for_____

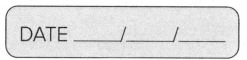

322. *Check In! What was journaling this week like for you? Where did you excel and where did you struggle? What new insights came up for you and how are you handling them? Which questions were more challenging than the others? Is there anything else that has happened this week that you'd like to sort through?*

_____

_____

_____

_____

_____

_____

_____

_____

_____

_____

Emotion of the day_____

I'm grateful for_____

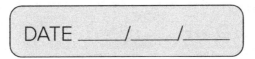

323. What do I want my life to look, sound, and feel like in 3 months, 1 year, 5 years?

_____

_____

_____

_____

_____

_____

_____

_____

_____

_____

_____

_____

DATE _____/_____/_____

Emotion of the day_____

I'm grateful for_____

324. How are the actions I'm making now leading me towards my long term goals?

_____

_____

_____

_____

_____

_____

_____

_____

_____

_____

_____

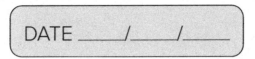

DATE _____ / _____ / _____

Emotion of the day _____

I'm grateful for _____

325. What does my best future self act and feel like?

_____

_____

_____

_____

_____

_____

_____

_____

_____

_____

_____

_____

_____

_____

DATE _____ / _____ / _____

Emotion of the day_____

I'm grateful for_____

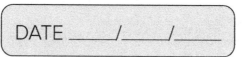

326. As my most ideal future self, what are my finances like?

_____

_____

_____

_____

_____

_____

_____

_____

_____

_____

_____

_____

_____

Emotion of the day_____

I'm grateful for_____

327. What about the future scares me? What skills do I have that I can utilize to move through that fear?

_____

_____

_____

_____

_____

_____

_____

_____

_____

_____

_____

_____

DATE ____/____/____

Emotion of the day _____

I'm grateful for _____

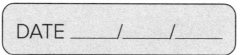

328. What adventures has my future self embarked on? What are they looking forward to?

_____

_____

_____

_____

_____

_____

_____

_____

_____

_____

_____

_____

_____

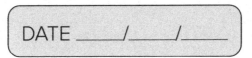

DATE _____/_____/_____

Emotion of the day_____

I'm grateful for_____

329. *Check In! What was journaling this week like for you? Where did you excel and where did you struggle? What new insights came up for you and how are you handling them? Which questions were more challenging than the others? Is there anything else that has happened this week that you'd like to sort through?*

_____

_____

_____

_____

_____

_____

_____

_____

_____

_____

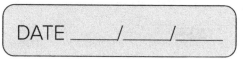

DATE _____/_____/_____

Emotion of the day_____

I'm grateful for_____

330. What are some unhelpful behaviors I would have to stop in order to become my favorite self?

_____

_____

_____

_____

_____

_____

_____

_____

_____

_____

_____

_____

_____

DATE _____ / _____ / _____

Emotion of the day_____

I'm grateful for_____

331. As my ideal future self, what is my mental and physical health like?

_____

_____

_____

_____

_____

_____

_____

_____

_____

_____

_____

_____

DATE ____/____/____

Emotion of the day _____

I'm grateful for _____

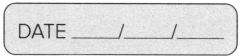

332. What is continuing to positively grow and evolve in my future self's life?

_____

_____

_____

_____

_____

_____

_____

_____

_____

_____

_____

_____

_____

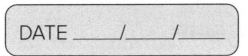

DATE _____/_____/_____

Emotion of the day_____

I'm grateful for_____

333. What is one thing I can do today to help out my tomorrow self?

_____

_____

_____

_____

_____

_____

_____

_____

_____

_____

_____

_____

_____

_____

DATE ____/____/____

Emotion of the day _____

I'm grateful for _____

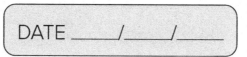

334. When am I the hardest on myself? E did I learn how to do that, and in what ways could I give myself more grace?

_____

_____

_____

_____

_____

_____

_____

_____

_____

_____

_____

_____

DATE ____/____/____

Emotion of the day_____

I'm grateful for_____

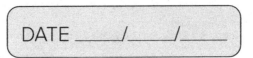

335. What advice would I give to myself future self?

_____
_____
_____
_____
_____
_____
_____
_____
_____
_____
_____
_____
_____

DATE _____/_____/_____

Emotion of the day _____

I'm grateful for _____

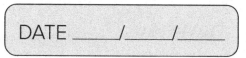

336. *Check In! What was journaling this week like for you? Where did you excel and where did you struggle? What new insights came up for you and how are you handling them? Which questions were more challenging than the others? Is there anything else that has happened this week that you'd like to sort through?*

_____

_____

_____

_____

_____

_____

_____

_____

_____

_____

Emotion of the day_____

I'm grateful for_____

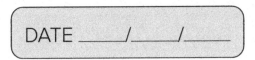

337. Describe what I love most about my future self. What are my favorite qualities? What kind of friend/partner/parent am I?

_____

_____

_____

_____

_____

_____

_____

_____

_____

_____

_____

_____

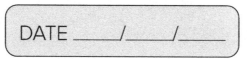

DATE _____ / _____ / _____

Emotion of the day_____

I'm grateful for_____

338. My dream life or dream career is a life characterized by...

_____

_____

_____

_____

_____

_____

_____

_____

_____

_____

_____

_____

_____

_____

DATE _____ / _____ / _____

Emotion of the day_____

I'm grateful for_____

339. I want to look forward to...

_____
_____
_____
_____
_____
_____
_____
_____
_____
_____
_____
_____
_____

DATE _____/_____/_____

Emotion of the day_____

I'm grateful for_____

340. How do I carry myself as my ideal future self? What energy am I giving off? How can I integrate that energy into my current self?

_____

_____

_____

_____

_____

_____

_____

_____

_____

_____

_____

_____

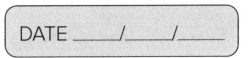

DATE ____/____/____

Emotion of the day_____

I'm grateful for_____

341. What would my healed future self say about how I currently console myself when I get upset?

_____

_____

_____

_____

_____

_____

_____

_____

_____

_____

_____

_____

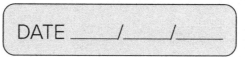

DATE _____/_____/_____

Emotion of the day_____

I'm grateful for_____

342. What would I like my relationship with food to look like in the future?

_____

_____

_____

_____

_____

_____

_____

_____

_____

_____

_____

_____

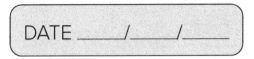

DATE ____/____/____

Emotion of the day_____

I'm grateful for_____

343. *Check In! What was journaling this week like for you? Where did you excel and where did you struggle? What new insights came up for you and how are you handling them? Which questions were more challenging than the others? Is there anything else that has happened this week that you'd like to sort through?*

_____

_____

_____

_____

_____

_____

_____

_____

_____

_____

_____

_____

DATE _____/_____/_____

Emotion of the day_____

I'm grateful for_____

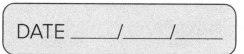

344. What adventures do I take while being my favorite version of myself?

_____

_____

_____

_____

_____

_____

_____

_____

_____

_____

_____

_____

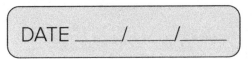

DATE ____/____/____

Emotion of the day _____

I'm grateful for _____

345. What do I want to do differently in my next relationship than I have in the past?

_____

_____

_____

_____

_____

_____

_____

_____

_____

_____

_____

_____

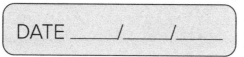

DATE _____/_____/_____

Emotion of the day_____

I'm grateful for_____

346. What does my ideal family life look like in the next 5 and 10 years?

_____
_____
_____
_____
_____
_____
_____
_____
_____
_____
_____

Emotion of the day_____

I'm grateful for_____

347. How would I like my relationship with my parents to evolve in the future?

_____

_____

_____

_____

_____

_____

_____

_____

_____

_____

_____

_____

DATE ____/____/____

Emotion of the day_____

I'm grateful for_____

348. How would I like my relationship with myself to evolve in the future? Have I already made progress with that relationship?

_____

_____

_____

_____

_____

_____

_____

_____

_____

_____

_____

_____

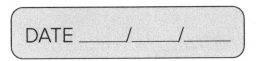
DATE _____ / _____ / _____

Emotion of the day _____

I'm grateful for _____

349. What would I like my relationship with money to look like in the future?

_____

_____

_____

_____

_____

_____

_____

_____

_____

_____

_____

_____

DATE ____/____/____

Emotion of the day _____

I'm grateful for _____

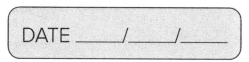

350. *Check In! What was journaling this week like for you? Where did you excel and where did you struggle? What new insights came up for you and how are you handling them? Which questions were more challenging than the others? Is there anything else that has happened this week that you'd like to sort through?*

_____

_____

_____

_____

_____

_____

_____

_____

_____

_____

Emotion of the day _____

I'm grateful for _____

351. In what ways can I start cultivating my ideal future self?

_____

_____

_____

_____

_____

_____

_____

_____

_____

_____

_____

_____

_____

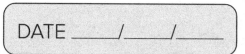

DATE ____/____/____

Emotion of the day _____

I'm grateful for _____

352. What new skills and knowledge does my future self have? How did I gain this information?

_____
_____
_____
_____
_____
_____
_____
_____
_____
_____
_____
_____

DATE ____/____/____

Emotion of the day _____

I'm grateful for _____

353. Something I'd like to achieve in the next year is...

_____

_____

_____

_____

_____

_____

_____

_____

_____

_____

_____

_____

_____

_____

DATE _____/_____/_____

Emotion of the day_____

I'm grateful for_____

354. How does the Patriarchy affect my life?

_____

_____

_____

_____

_____

_____

_____

_____

_____

_____

_____

_____

_____

DATE ____/____/____

Emotion of the day_____

I'm grateful for_____

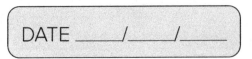

355. What does my future self value most in life? How does that align with what I currently value?

_____
_____
_____
_____
_____
_____
_____
_____
_____
_____
_____
_____
_____

DATE ____/____/____

Emotion of the day_____

I'm grateful for_____

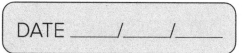

356. What would my healed future self advise me to do in order to get through this present phase of my life?

_____

_____

_____

_____

_____

_____

_____

_____

_____

_____

_____

_____

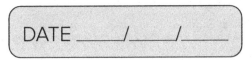

DATE _____ / _____ / _____

Emotion of the day _____

I'm grateful for _____

357. *Check In! What was journaling this week like for you? Where did you excel and where did you struggle? What new insights came up for you and how are you handling them? Which questions were more challenging than the others? Is there anything else that has happened this week that you'd like to sort through?*

_____

_____

_____

_____

_____

_____

_____

_____

_____

_____

_____

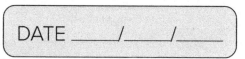

DATE _____ / _____ / _____

Emotion of the day _____

I'm grateful for _____

358. How do I see my current problems coming to a resolution in the future?

_____

_____

_____

_____

_____

_____

_____

_____

_____

_____

_____

_____

_____

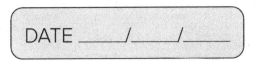

DATE ____ / ____ / ____

Emotion of the day_____

I'm grateful for_____

☼   ☁   ⚡   🌈   ❄

359. What is something I can reward myself with once I finish this journal?

_____
_____
_____
_____
_____
_____
_____
_____
_____
_____
_____
_____
_____

DATE _____/_____/_____

Emotion of the day _____

I'm grateful for _____

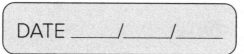

360. How does it feel to only have 1 more week of questions to get through before you've finished this journal?

_____

_____

_____

_____

_____

_____

_____

_____

_____

_____

_____

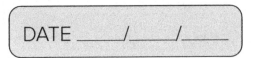

DATE _____/_____/_____

Emotion of the day _____

I'm grateful for _____

361. What have I accomplished in this past year that I didn't think I would have? How does that make me feel?

_____
_____
_____
_____
_____
_____
_____
_____
_____
_____
_____
_____
_____

DATE ____ / ____ / ____

Emotion of the day_____

I'm grateful for_____

362. What actions or activities make me feel purposeful? How often do I participate in those activities?

_____

_____

_____

_____

_____

_____

_____

_____

_____

_____

_____

_____

DATE _____ / _____ / _____

Emotion of the day_____

I'm grateful for_____

363. What have I learned about myself by engaging in this crazy adventure?

_____

_____

_____

_____

_____

_____

_____

_____

_____

_____

_____

_____

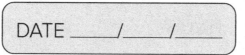

DATE _____/_____/_____

Emotion of the day_____

I'm grateful for_____

364. *Check In! What was journaling this week like for you? Where did you excel and where did you struggle? What new insights came up for you and how are you handling them? Which questions were more challenging than the others? Is there anything else that has happened this week that you'd like to sort through?*

_____

_____

_____

_____

_____

_____

_____

_____

_____

_____

DATE ____ / ____ / ____

Emotion of the day_____

I'm grateful for_____

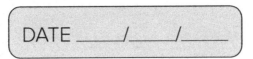

365. What do I want to do more of in the future that will continue my healing journey?

_____

_____

_____

_____

_____

_____

_____

_____

_____

_____

_____

_____

Emotion of the day_____

I'm grateful for_____

366. Holy shit... you're fucking done!!! How does it feel?!?!

_____

_____

_____

_____

_____

_____

_____

_____

_____

_____

_____

_____

_____

_____

journaling book citations

Kolk, V. D., & Bessel, A. (2014). *The body keeps the score: brain, mind, and body in the healing of trauma.* https://ci.nii.ac.jp/ncid/BB19708339

https://www.ncbi.nlm.nih.gov/pmc/articles/PMC2907136/#:~:text=The%20prefrontal%20cortex%20(PFC)%20intelligently,brain%20regions%20(BOX%201).

https://psychcentral.com/anxiety/vagus-nerve-cooling-anxiety#the-vagus-nerve

https://notesbythalia.com/future-self-journaling-prompts/

https://www.teachersnotepad.com/writing-prompts-about-the-future/

https://ambitiouslyalexa.com/future-self-journal-prompts/

https://www.indeed.com/career-advice/career-development/confidence-questions

https://authenticallydel.com/questions-for-improved-self-confidence/

https://thedailyguru.com/self-esteem-questions/

https://steppingstonetherapy.org/conversation-starters/

https://www.timeperiodsgame.com